COUPLES

THE MOST INTIMATE ACT BETWEEN A

WHO

MAN AND A WOMAN

PRAY

HUSBAND AND WIFE

SQUIRE RUSHNELL
LOUISE DuART

THOMAS NELSON
Since 1798

NASHVILLE   DALLAS   MEXICO CITY   RIO DE JANEIRO

Published in Nashville, Tennessee, by Thomas Nelson. Thomas Nelson is a registered trademark of Thomas Nelson, Inc.

Thomas Nelson, Inc. titles may be purchased in bulk for educational, business, fund-raising, or sales promotional use. For information, please e-mail SpecialMarkets@ThomasNelson.com.

Couples Who Pray is an official publication of SQuire Rushnell's The 40 Day Prayer Challenge™.

Unless otherwise noted, Scripture quotations are from the Holy Bible: New International Version®. © 1973, 1978, 1984 by the International Bible Society. Used by permission of Zondervan Publishing House. All rights reserved.

Scripture quotations marked CEV are from the Contemporary English Version. © 1991 by the American Bible Society. Used by permission.

Scripture quotations marked NCV are from the New Century Version®. © 2005 by Thomas Nelson, Inc. Used by permission. All rights reserved.

Scripture quotations marked KJV are from the Holy Bible, King James Version.

Scripture quotations marked NASB are from the New American Standard Bible®, © by The Lockman Foundation 1960, 1962, 1963, 1968, 1971, 1972, 1973, 1975, 1977, 1995. Used by permission.

Scripture quotations marked NKJV are from the New King James Version®. © 1982 by Thomas Nelson, Inc. Used by permission. All rights reserved.

Scripture quotations marked NLT are from the Holy Bible, New Living Translation. © 1996. Used by permission of Tyndale House Publishers, Inc., Wheaton, Illinois 60189. All rights reserved.

Scripture quotations marked MSG are from *The Message* by Eugene H. Peterson. © 1993, 1994, 1995, 1996, 2000. Used by permission of NavPress Publishing Group. All rights reserved.

ISBN 978-0-7852-3196-7 (trade paper)

LIBRARY OF CONGRESS CATALOGING-IN-PUBLICATION DATA

RUSHNELL, SQUIRE D., 1938–
    COUPLES WHO PRAY : THE MOST INTIMATE ACT BETWEEN A MAN AND A WOMAN / SQUIRE RUSHNELL AND LOUISE DUART.
        P. CM.
    INCLUDES BIBLIOGRAPHICAL REFERENCES.
    ISBN 978-0-7852-2794-6 (HARDCOVER)
        1. MARRIED PEOPLE—RELIGIOUS LIFE. 2. PRAYER—CHRISTIANITY. I. DUART, LOUISE. II. TITLE.
    BV4596.M3R87 2007
    248.3'208655—DC22

                                                                    2007044354

Printed in the United States of America
11 12 13 14 15 **RRD** 5 4 3 2 1

To you and all couples who,
by adopting the powerful
principles of this book, fuel
The New Movement 2 Pray—measurably
changing lives and igniting joy,
evidenced by declining divorce rates
throughout the world.

CONTENTS

INTRODUCTION

This book comes with a warning:

BE AWARE
READING THIS BOOK WILL
CHANGE YOUR MARRIAGE!

THE MOST INTIMATE ACT

Men—most of you will want to know that the most intimate act between a man and a woman will greatly enhance the frequency and ecstasy of lovemaking.

Women—most of you will want to know that the most intimate act will greatly expand meaningful communication with your partner almost overnight.

And, if you are like most of the couples who tell their stories in this book, you will soon realize a remarkable elevation in mutual respect. You'll find yourself agreeing with each other more, and your gauge of happiness will absolutely soar!

You may ask:

- *What do I have to do to get these results?*

  Invest five minutes a day, minimum, praying with your partner.

- *What is the cost?*

  Commit to a pattern of daily prayer for an initial period of forty days.

- *Is this some kind of new discovery—a long-hidden secret?*

  No. The principles discussed here are found in the instruction manual to life; you'll find it in the top drawer of just about every hotel room in America: the Bible.

- *Why is this called* "the most intimate act between a man and a woman"?

  Name one thing—from sharing a toothbrush to soaking in a hot tub—that is truly more intimate than simultaneously exposing your vulnerabilities to your spouse and your Creator.

- *How can I trust your claims?*

  Astonishing research—conducted by Gallup and Baylor University—unveiled in these pages, substantiates our premise, over and over.

- *How come I've never heard about this before?*

  It is true, the vast majority of couples—even Christian couples—have not been told about, let alone practiced, the extraordinary power and intimacy of joint prayer for a few minutes every day. If they did, divorce rates would plummet and permanent smiles would be etched on the faces of millions of men and women.

The most intimate act is prayer.

As you will learn in the pages that follow, couples who bare themselves before God in prayer for a minimum of five minutes a day for forty days have extraordinary results:

- Satisfaction in lovemaking soars.
- Spousal communication elevates.
- Respect rises.
- Agreement becomes the norm.
- Happiness is a way of life.

Your marriage can have the same results. And that is a promise.

WHAT QUALIFIES US TO WRITE THIS BOOK

When we look back at our past marriages, we realize that there was a cloud of sadness that always lingered. We didn't have the freedom to share our innermost thoughts and concerns with our spouses. We were playing the role of happily married couples but there was always the feeling of emptiness. Here is how we came to this point:

Louise: I was living on the West Coast, going through the motions of life, an empty shell, wearing a fake face. I attended church every Sunday morning, all by myself. My husband wasn't a believer. As an impressionist, I study people for a living. There I'd sit, studying couples. It wasn't hard to determine which were which—those who simply *existed* in a dormant marriage versus those whose love for each other simply radiated.

SQuire: I was living on the East Coast, drifting through a similar façade; a failure at marriage for the second time. At a little country church, where I'd go alone, I'd gaze at a couple who always sat three rows ahead of me. I envied those two—the way their shoulders touched, the brightness in their eyes as they glanced and smiled at each other. I deduced they were communicating in some secret language. They were. It was the language of love. For me, love was a distant, unfulfilled dream.

Louise: Later on, I was in New York appearing in a Broadway show. I was no longer married—my husband had run off with another woman.

SQuire: I was also no longer married and spent weekends with my brain-injured son, Grant. Due to a last-minute change of schedule for an out-of-town trip, I was able to stay in New York and take my boy to a Broadway show. Looking in the paper I said, "Hey, my old friend Louise DuArt is appearing in a show called *Dreamstuff.*" I explained that twenty years earlier I'd hired her for a TV show.

Louise: When SQuire sent his card backstage and asked if I wanted to have coffee after the show, my heart skipped.

SQuire: We had coffee that day, and almost every day since.

Louise: After meeting SQuire for coffee, I called my mother and said, "Do you remember SQuire Rushnell, the guy who used to run ABC Children's Television? Well, I'm going to marry him. Does he know? No. Not yet.

SQuire: When we were married in that little country church where I had mourned for the love I never had, I knew God was delivering me a gift like none other. By the way, the incredible godwink was this: the day my out-of-town trip was canceled was also the same day for the closing performance of Louise's Broadway show. Now, that's what we call divine alignment!

Louise: I don't remember when we actually started praying together, do you, honey?

SQuire: No, I don't. But inviting God into our conversations was a natural progression. I know I was a bit wooden at first. But pretty soon, I felt we were three—you, me, and God. That's when that ancient text made sense: a couple is like two strands of a rope that, when woven together with God, becomes unbreakable.

Louise: Right after we were married in October 2000, Gary Smalley, a wonderfully respected marriage advisor, suggested that we put our experiences together for marriage seminars.

SQuire: And what was born was a show we called *Everything I Know About Wrecking Relationships* . . .

Louise: . . . *I Learned in My Last Marriage.*

SQuire: Why were we qualified? We'd *been there and done that.* We'd endured every bit of pain you could imagine. Yet here we were—two people who had emerged from the darkness and glowed with the kind of joy that only comes from above.

Louise: It was at the performance of those events that so many couples told us that they pray individually—but they'd never even considered praying together.

SQuire: No one . . . no church, nobody had ever explained to them the extraordinary merits of a husband and wife praying together.

Louise: And when we began researching, we realized that not only do extremely few couples pray together, but the data and institutional support is almost nonexistent.

SQuire: Louise and I discovered that we had unveiled a divine inheritance—a revelation that needs to be shared with everyone!"

Louise: SQuire and I pray every single morning and often at other times of the day as well. Now our lives are far from empty. We are rich with the amazing gift of unconditional love. It is a love that is not conjured up. It is real and everlasting. It's a fire that never goes out. It grows with each day that we're together. Our purpose in our marriage is to serve each other and love each other as much as we can. What we found is that we can't out-love each other because God's well never runs dry. He replenishes it with more love. Human love can't offer that. Only God's love can do that.

SQuire: Our hope is that you, too, will grasp the joy of a relationship that God intended for you. By committing to pray together a minimum of five minutes a day for forty days, you will be astonished by the ecstasy that follows.

Louise: We're asking you to give The 40 Day Prayer Challenge a try. We can boldly guarantee that if you and your partner are sincere in wanting a better relationship, you can be sure that God will do great things!

CELEBRITIES SHARE INTIMATE STORIES

To underscore the merits of our message, some of America's most famous people shared their stories with us for this book. Their stories will take you places you've never been—into private conversations about the most intimate acts in their lives. For instance:

- When Denzel Washington goes off to work as a Hollywood leading man, how does Pauletta, his wife of twenty-five years, protect the fortress of their marriage?
- What is the secret that makes Kathie Lee and Frank Gifford's marriage "better than ever"?
- What can you learn from the way Tracie Hamilton and her husband, Olympic gold medalist Scott Hamilton, faced a crisis that will help you dramatically change your marriage?

But that's not all; read on!

REAL PEOPLE, REAL COUPLES . . . LIFE-CHANGING STORIES

To exemplify the merits of The 40 Day Prayer Challenge, we invited some two dozen couples to take the challenge, then tell us what happened. They will be your guides. Step by step, their insights will help you to take one of the most life-changing experiences into which you have ever entered.

THE PLAYBILL

Following is a cast list—in order of appearance—of the couples, celebrities included, who participated in The 40 Day Prayer Challenge (and whose stories made the final edit of this book). We are deeply grateful to each of them for the extraordinary wit and wisdom they have shared.

- Mari Falcone and Bill Cantos, a highly musical couple, have been married fourteen years and live in Los Angeles. Mari was trained as a concert pianist and has composed, conducted, or directed for performers such as Donna Summer, Amy Grant, and Debby Boone. Bill has a master's degree in music and frequently performs with Phil Collins. Bill's recent album, *Love Wins*, has received numerous kudos for not only the singing performances but also his compositions. Mari and Bill's praying together has opened amazing new avenues.

- Donna Summer and Bruce Sudano, married twenty-seven years, have prayed together and worked together right from the beginning. Donna is the legendary singer, songwriter, and artist best known for a string of dance hits in the 1970s, earning her the title of Queen of Disco. Bruce is a respected music producer, singer, and cocomposer of some of Donna's greatest hits. They live in Nashville, Tennessee.

- Tiffany and Matt McClain, young marrieds—two years—are exhilarated by the joys and struggles of building careers and family. Tiffany is a producer for CBN. Matt has a robust home painting business in the Virginia Beach area. Biggest news of the moment: they're expecting their first baby! Joint prayer has been very effective in getting them through some difficult issues.

- Robin and Dave Taney from Rochester have been happily married for two years. During this time they have served as foster parents and faced the difficulties of losing a parent. Dave has also sustained an injury resulting from a medical procedure, which has kept him out of work for several months. Normally, he's a weekend drummer with a weekday career in the corporate world. Robin, a former CNN producer, is an Internet writer and producer for travel and attractions. Praying together opened a whole new chapter in the Taneys' marriage.

- Pauletta and Denzel Washington, considered to be one of Hollywood's most stable couples, have been married twenty-five years. Pauletta was an accomplished stage performer when the two of them met during the shooting of the film *Wilma*, which provided Denzel his first screen role. Pauletta put her career on pause to raise three children while Denzel went on to win two Academy Awards as a top box-office leading man and become a film director. Prayer is mortar in their marriage.

- Donna and Joe Daniels have lived in Atlantic City during their twelve-year marriage. Donna is a talented choreographer and director who somehow balances her overcrowded roles of wife and mother of an eight-year-old with running a performing arts studio. Joe is a retired police officer whose landscaping business keeps him going from morning to night. "We're two ships in the night, hoping to bump into each other," says Donna. When they do, they resume praying together.

- Shellie and Dan Dunlap have been "embracing the journey" of matrimony for twenty-one years. With ownership of banks in Phoenix and Iowa, the couple now lives near Boston where their teenage daughter attends a performing arts high school. Joint prayer—not uncommon for them—was even more helpful when it became disciplined.

- Patsy and Les Clairmont have been married forty-five years and have homes in Texas and Michigan. Much of the time, Patsy is on the road with Women of Faith®, speaking before audiences of 10,000 to 40,000. The Clairmonts' revelations about joint prayer came like a bolt of lightning, changing the course of their lives.

- Anqunette Jamison and Dan Urban, married two years, live near Boston. Both grapple with career stresses and uncertainties; she's a television anchorwoman, and he's a chef manager. Praying together was a new and rewarding experience for the couple.

- Ethel and Michael Patrick have been married twenty-five years. Ethel has had a rewarding career as a nurse and is a mother of three. Michael has had a robust career as a network television journalist, covering five U.S. presidents and witnessing many of the vital news events that shaped the end of the past century. He is currently dean of communications at Regent University in Virginia Beach. His goal is to make a lasting redemptive difference in a world that is literally dying to hear and experience the truth.

- Cristina Ferrare and Tony Thomopoulos have been married twenty years. Cristina's career has spanned being a fashion model, actress, author, and television talk-show host. Tony has also had a diverse career, holding the position of president of ABC Entertainment and Amblin television. He's the man to thank for the original placement of NBC's highly acclaimed program *ER*, in addition to several other successful series on network television. Tony is currently a founder and partner of Promise Media Productions. Cristina and Tony live in Los Angeles with their children.

- Janice and Jeff Wooden live on the beautiful island of Martha's Vineyard where Jeff serves on the MV Commission as administrator. Janice is an interior designer who works with Past & Presents, a popular Edgartown store. They've been married twenty-seven years and offer this counsel: "If you think you have a good marriage now, praying with your partner will make it even better."

- Kathie Lee and Frank Gifford have been married twenty years. Kathie Lee is best known as the cohost of *Live with*

Regis and Kathie Lee. She recently began working in musical theatre. She wrote and produced *Under the Bridge,* which played off-Broadway. In 2007 she received wonderful reviews for *Saving Aimee* in the Washington D.C. area and contributed several favorite songs to the musical *Hats.* Frank Gifford began his NFL career with the New York Giants, winning the Most Valuable Player award, and is enshrined in the Pro Football Hall of Fame. Frank became well known as a commentator for ABC's *Monday Night Football.* He and Kathie Lee have two children and live in Connecticut.

• Joey and Sharon Paul have had a wonderful marriage for more than two decades, exemplifying strong support for each other. Joey has been in the publishing world for most of his career, first with Word, Inc., later with Integrity, and currently as a prominent publisher for Thomas Nelson.

• Tracie and Scott Hamilton have been married for three years and are the parents of one child with another on the way. Prior to their marriage, Tracie was a prominent dietary executive in the L.A. food business. In 1981 Scott won the gold medal in the World Figure Skating Championship. He won gold again in 1982 and 1983 at the U.S. and World Championships and won the gold medal at the 1984 Winter Olympics. After turning professional, he toured with Ice Capades for two years then created "Scott Hamilton's American Tour," later renamed "Stars on Ice," which he coproduced and performed in for fifteen years. The Hamiltons live in Franklin, Tennessee.

- Patti and Gavin MacLeod have been married and remarried for twenty years. Patti's career started as a singer and dancer while Gavin went from playing the wisecracking Murray Slaughter on the CBS sitcom *The Mary Tyler Moore Show* to playing the captain of *The Love Boat* on ABC. After Patti and Gavin were divorced and remarried, they together hosted a talk show for Trinity Broadcasting Network entitled *Back on Course: A Ministry for Marriages.*

- Angela and John Griffin, married eight years, describe themselves as "two peas in a pod," living in Woodstock, Georgia. Both love the life of entrepreneurs. John is the founder of *Christian Living Magazine* and has been an advisor to Angela's very successful real-estate company.

- Paula and Jeff Friedrichsen have been married ten years. Paula is a speaker and the author of *The Man You Always Wanted Is the One You Already Have.* She and Jeff, who is semi-retired, live in northern California with their children, an adorable lapdog, and a twenty-pound cat.

- Kay and Rick Warren live in Southern California where they built Saddleback Church into one of the nation's largest megachurches. *Time* magazine named Rick one of "15 World Leaders Who Mattered Most in 2004" and in 2005 one of the "100 Most Influential People in the World." Rick's book *The Purpose Driven Life* has sold more than thirty million copies, the best-selling hardback book in American history. As philanthropists, Rick and Kay give away 90 percent of their income.

• Linda and Glen Gillis recently celebrated forty-two years of marriage but consider it their "third" anniversary, following marriage therapy. The couple spent twenty-five years in the Chicago area raising three children. Glen retired in 2002 from computer consulting, and they moved to Arizona. Linda will soon retire from many years working for the Lutheran Church and will continue to write and present spiritual retreats. Next year they'll be off in their RV, visiting their daughters on each coast, and both agree that their faith in God helped them discover their new relationship.

• Mary Ellen Walden and Jimi Gibbs live on two islands: Long Island and Martha's Vineyard. Mary Ellen is a real-estate entrepreneur while Jimi is a much-in-demand carpenter, handyman, and estate caretaker.

• Cathy and Ken Campbell have been married for thirty years. Ken is a retired pastor, studying for his doctoral degree in theology before kick-starting his next career. Cathy is in the ministry of encouraging people with the hopeful message of God's power and grace through life's difficult challenges. They recently moved to Austin, Texas, to be near one of their two children and several grandchildren.

• Luci Swindoll comes from a family of great communicators. For more than a decade, she's been one of the founding members of Women of Faith®, reaching more than 400,000 attendees a year. To hear Luci tell it, joy is everywhere . . . you just have to know how to look. And her life proves it. She found joy working as a corporate executive at Mobil Oil, singing with the Dallas Opera, serving as vice president of public relations for her brother Chuck Swindoll's ministry, and now traveling as perennial world speaker with Women of Faith®. Luci also finds joy when she gets to return to her art studio-library-home in Frisco, Texas.

SECTION

MAJOR BENEFITS OF COUPLES
PRAYING TOGETHER

NAKED TRUTH:
MARRIAGE'S MOST INTIMATE ACT

Honestly, can you think of *any* act *more* intimate than joining together in a quiet place, holding hands in prayer, and allowing your soul to be bare naked before God?

This is our pledge: entering into this act of intimacy on a daily basis with the one person you love more than any other will take you to a level of joy and satisfaction that you simply will not believe.

Your love life will be better, your communication better. Your whole life will be so much better.

You'll find yourself beginning every prayer session saying "thank you" for this new life-changing experience.

Research Revealed—Then, Step-By-Step

In section two of this book, we'll take you step-by-step through the process of The 40 Day Prayer Challenge—asking you to commit to praying together for a minimum of five minutes a day for forty days.

For the moment, though, we want to reveal some very rare but incredible research on what happens to couples who pray, exemplified through true-life stories about couples just like you who have experienced the ecstasy that we've been talking about. We start with the two areas of primary interest for men and women—the effect of prayer on lovemaking, addressed in this chapter, and its effect on spousal communication, addressed in the next chapter.

Life-Changing Lovemaking

Since they have been praying together, "Lovemaking is better," say Mari and Bill almost simultaneously.

"It has to be," adds Mari enthusiastically. "It's all about intimacy. I've never felt greater closeness to God than when Bill and I pray."

"When we're in communication with God," adds Bill, "God is in communication with us. And when you submit yourselves to God as a couple, you really see the difference."

Mari Falcone—the spirited, redheaded conductor for Donna Summer and many others—and Bill Cantos, Mari's handsome, bearded husband—a composer, singer, and keyboard artist in his own right—had been madly in love and married nearly fifteen years.

Before taking The 40 Day Prayer Challenge, they had occasionally prayed together but not with regularity. "We weren't committed to daily prayer," admits Bill.

By the end of the challenge, Mari's excitement was uncontainable: "We couldn't imagine that praying together would be so life changing. What an incredible experience!"

"When you're with God you're being as honest and unguarded as you ever get—you're being the best person you can be," deduces Bill. "And when you're with God *together*, you experience each other in that intimate, unguarded way. It allows you to have more of a heart for each other . . ."

"And that affects lovemaking," continues Mari. "When you pray, you are vulnerable. A man thinks he always needs to show a woman his strength—that he has it all together—but when I hear Bill asking God for help, I actually feel *more* secure. As a woman, I know if he asks for God's help, he'll receive it, and that makes me more secure."

"It's interesting . . . what a man perceives as weakness, the woman sees as strength," interprets Bill.

"Prayer definitely affects lovemaking," reaffirms Mari, as Bill nods in agreement. "The man says 'whoopee,' but the woman sees a different side of her husband that takes lovemaking to a whole other level."

Bill sums up their feelings about The 40 Day Prayer Challenge: "I was surprised by the effect. I thought it would be positive, but never imagined how God would keep on blessing us."

"When the forty days were over, we stopped praying for a

few days," confesses Mari, "and we noticed our bickering level went back up. During the forty days, bickering had been nonexistent."

"Praying together is a daily discipline," concludes Bill.

"But who knew that it would be so incredibly life changing," repeats Mari excitedly.

DONNA AND BRUCE ON INTIMACY

"Praying together bonds us," says Donna Summer. "I can't really explain the way it bonds us . . . it's so deep and healthy . . . I can't imagine living without it."

Donna and her husband, Bruce Sudano—who has a long history in the music business as a singer, songwriter, and producer—have been married for twenty-seven years. Bruce has cowritten some of Donna's most memorable songs. He travels with her as part of the touring show and oversees the day-to-day family business. Donna and Bruce have been praying together from the very beginning of their marriage. "We were attracted to each other because of our faith," says Bruce.

Prayer is the spiritual glue in their marriage. "Telltale signs will creep in, and one of us will say, 'We need to pray,'" he adds.

"I don't know how couples survive when they don't have this common ground," continues Donna, "this little room they can slide into and hide away with each other. It is a different thing than sex."

"Praying with your husband lets him into your inner sanctum, and when he can dwell there, he gets to really know you. That's what prayer does for me and my husband: it enables me to know him."

Bruce agrees. "When you are in prayer, you talk to God about things and let your true heart come through . . . almost subliminal communication between husband and wife."

Donna remains in thought about prayer being a special place for a couple. "It's a place of arbitration. I know he doesn't want to go into that place with any sense of untruth. When we enter that space together, we are both putting down our weapons and standing there spiritually and emotionally naked. We say, 'God, this is what I need . . . this is what I feel insecure about.'"

As with most couples, Donna and Bruce have found that joint prayer is such an intimate act that all feelings become transparent.

"It is a humbling thing to know if my husband feels insecure about something," says Donna. "As a woman, it makes me want to nurture that place. Vice versa, when he knows something is a deep wound for me, then he doesn't trample on that place in me anymore. He prays for that place in me."

"It is so healing and so healthy," they agree in unison.

I recommend you look at the word *intimacy* in a new way. Think of the word as: into-me-see.[1]

—PENNY BANUCHI

THE RESEARCH THAT SURPRISED THE RESEARCHERS

In the late 1980s there was a flurry of publishing activity on human sexuality, ignited in part by the popularity of *The Hite Report on Male and Female Sexuality* and by the rising concerns about promiscuity and the spread of AIDS. As a result, the prestigious magazine *Psychology Today* decided to commission its own study on marriage to see if there had been a major shift in martial fidelity.

Called "Love and Marriage," the study was carried out by Gallup Poll, one of the nation's most prominent research firms. The results were then published in a 1991 book by Andrew Greeley called *Faithful Attraction*.

Greeley wrote, "I can only say at the end of this research I am pleasantly surprised at how much resilience and vitality there is in American marriage."[2]

Although that may have been an outcome that was unanticipated by Gallup and *Psychology Today* editors, the most astonishing aspect of the Love and Marriage study was buried within—the revelation about couples who pray: "Whether they pray often together is a very powerful correlate of marital happiness," said Greeley, "the most powerful we have yet discovered."[3]

For the purposes of writing this book, we asked Byron Johnson, who heads up Baylor University's Institute for Studies of Religion, to reevaluate the Gallup study's findings on couples who pray. His report with Jerry Park, assistant professor of sociology at Baylor, was indeed astonishing.

Byron Johnson advises readers to "please keep in mind that the comparisons in this study are among respondents who said they pray together with their spouses 'a lot' versus those who pray 'sometimes.' Considering that the following data between those two groups is so distinct, imagine what the results would be if we were able to compare the pray-a-lot respondents with the vast segment of the general population which 'never' pray together."

According to Jerry Park, "People who pray with their spouses a lot, compared to people who pray with their spouses sometimes, find that their lives and marriages improve, often with astonishing results."

The following data provides the evidence—couples who pray sometimes versus those who pray a lot:

HAPPINESS
- 60% vs. 78% are likely to say their "marriage is happy" —a difference of 18%.
- 73% vs. 92% who are "satisfied with sex a great deal" report they are "very happy with their marriage." That's a 19% distinction.
- 59% vs. 72% say they are "very happy" in general.
- 74% vs. 91% say, "My spouse is my best friend."

FAMILY AND CHILDREN
- 64% vs. 75% say they "agree on how children should be raised."
- 38% vs. 54% are satisfied with their family life "a very great deal."

MONEY MATTERS
- 58% vs. 69% rate their agreement on financial matters as "very good."

DISAGREEMENTS

- 72% vs. 83% say agreement with their spouse on basic values is "very good."
- 66% vs. 75% have a "very good" ability to disagree with their partner without threatening their relationship—an elevation of 9%.
- 35% vs. 57% say, "My spouse is a good compromiser."
- 65% vs. 86% "try to make their marriage better"—a significant 21% distinction.

COMMUNICATION

- 42% vs. 53% of these couples say they "try to talk together without interruption."

RESPECT

- 59% vs. 77% say, "My spouse makes me feel important."
- 56% vs. 75% conversely report that "my spouse would say I make him/her feel important."

DELIGHT

- 39% vs. 69%—a huge 30% difference—agree that "my spouse delights in me."

LOVEMAKING

- 67% vs. 82%—an elevation of 15%—say they are "satisfied with their sex life" a "very great deal" or a "great deal."
- 52% vs. 72%—20% more—say the "quantity and quality of lovemaking is very good."
- 69% vs. 78% apply the term "ecstasy" to lovemaking.

- 42% vs. 63% say, "My spouse is romantic."
- 48% vs. 65% contend "my spouse is a skillful lover."
- 49% vs. 68% say they "feel spiritual joy after lovemaking." That's an increase of 19% as a direct correlation to praying together.

STABILITY OF MARRIAGE

- 76% vs. 92% rate their confidence in the stability of their marriage as "very good."
- 81% vs. 93% agree if they had to do it all over again, they "would marry the same person."
- 0% vs. 0% is the fear of divorce—virtually eliminated in both groups—among couples who are "satisfied with sex a great deal."
- 4% vs. 2% is the fear of divorce among people who are "satisfied *less than* a very great deal with their sex lives."[4]

EXTRAORDINARY DATA

The Gallup data uncovered by Baylor University's analysis is nothing short of extraordinary in our view.

Virtually every one of the categories measuring marital bliss escalated significantly when couples simply prayed together a lot versus sometimes. In some cases the swing was 15 to 30 percent.

Here's another astonishing factor to consider: this study is the only one we've been able to locate in which the merits of couples praying together have been measured. Our friends at Baylor University's Institute for Studies of Religion have not researched this before nor have those at Barna Research or any other firm insofar as we've been able to determine.

SMALL ACT—HUGE CHANGE

As Byron Johnson mentioned earlier, imagine if this study had compared couples who pray a lot with those who never pray together. The fact is most couples do not pray together. Even most Christian couples do not pray together often—only 4 percent, by one informal account. More surprising, many pastors and their wives fail to practice the habit of daily prayer.

"Most couples tell me that they very rarely pray together, with the exception of meal-time," says Steve Carr, marital advisor with the Covenant Keepers.[5]

Yet we can see from the results of the foregoing studies that a very small investment—as little as five minutes a day—can deliver huge dividends for your marriage, drastically improving its course and, as a result, changing your life.

Greeley's analysis of the Gallup study concluded: "Prayer . . . is a much more powerful predictor of marital satisfaction than frequency of sexual intercourse—though the *combination* of sex and prayer correlates with very, very high levels of marital fulfillment."[6]

A PERSONAL POSTSCRIPT ON LOVEMAKING

The only time you will find the three-letter word *s-e-x* in this book is when it is quoted from other sources. Our perception is that sex is a physical act that may or may not involve love. Lovemaking, on the other hand, is a total experience, which is exquisite because love is what it's all about.

LOVEMAKING AND MARRIAGE

In his "Ten Tips for Making Marriage Fun," Dr. Robert Schuller says lovemaking "was meant by God, our Creator, to be life's greatest pleasure. Nobody has ever enjoyed sex more than those who have kept it within the confines of the marriage commitment."[7]

While research on the outcome of couples praying together is very rare, there is ample discussion on the connection between marital satisfaction and a couple's commitment before God to be faithful to each other.

This boils down to the value that the two of you have placed on the covenant of marriage into which you have entered.

COVENANT VERSUS MARRIAGE CERTIFICATE

What's the difference between a covenant and a marriage certificate? The latter can be acquired from town hall. It's an impersonal series of words and signatures on a piece of paper, as routine as getting a driver's license. But a marriage covenant is an agreement between you and your partner and God. The town clerk may forget all about you the next day. God won't.

Famed Hollywood pastor Jack Hayford emphasizes the seriousness of the expression of promises between two people by making this big statement: "The covenant of marriage is the single most important human bond that holds all of God's work on the planet together." He goes on to say, "No wonder the Lord is passionate about the sanctity of marriage and the stability of the home. This covenant of marriage is based on the covenant God has made with us."[8]

THE EXPRESSION OF LOVE

"The first time we had a real long prayer together we made love and it was really different . . . and it has been ever since," says Tiffany as she and her husband, Matt, approach their second anniversary.

"When we give ourselves to each other as husband and wife, it's as if God rewards us," she concludes.

Matt agrees, adding that their overall communication was aided by their daily prayer together . . . that they discovered things about each other that they had not clearly comprehended before.

"I knew she wanted a baby," says Matt, "but as I heard her pouring her heart out to God . . . and how serious she was . . . it became real to me."

Tiffany, in turn, notes that things she had not known Matt was concerned about emerged in their prayer time. "Matt came from a background where feelings were not expressed openly. But when he is speaking directly to the Lord, I feel that he's deeply sincere. It's nice to see that side of him . . . and that contributes to our expressions to each other during lovemaking."

PRAYER AND CONTENTMENT

"Do I think there's a connection between lovemaking and prayer? Of course I do," says Robin earnestly. "Dave is more selfless in his whole demeanor—there's an authenticity in his manner; he wants to make me happy and I find that very sexy."

With a modest rejoinder, Dave says, "Unfortunately I had surgery during our forty days, but, no question, prayer definitely made a difference. We'll keep it going."

Dave's surgical procedure to remove a cyst unfortunately injured a nerve, thereby protracting his recovery.

"We're still not as physical because he's still in pain, but I'm very content," affirms Robin.

2

PRAYER AND COMMUNICATION

START WITH YOUR FRAME OF MIND

Communication between a man and a woman is vitally important to a successful marriage, and it begins with your frame of mind.

There's a natural inclination for two people to think about marriage as a 50/50 arrangement, each person contributing one-half to the effort. But the natural outcome of that thinking is to begin tabulating a scorecard in your head, keeping lists of how much you think you have contributed versus your partner.

Keeping a relationship tally of any sort is a bad idea.

Men usually don't expect women to pick up the check at a restaurant 50 percent of the time. Or drive the car 50 percent of the time.

Women usually don't expect men to do 50 percent of the cooking and laundry.

Fact is, there are many instances in the average family that automatically assume one gender will contribute more than the other. *So let's establish this premise: each of you should expect to put in much more than your share to make your marriage work.*

PAULETTA WASHINGTON— THE WOMAN'S INFLUENCE

"Eighty-five percent of the success or failure of your marriage is on *you!*" said my mother firmly.

I was in total shock at what I thought to be the most ridiculous, antiquated statement I'd ever heard from my mom.

I replied, "Mom, please . . . this is a new day. It's 50/50."

"It's *not* 50/50," retorted Mom. "And if you think it is, you're in deep trouble. You should most certainly rethink your decision to get married."

"But invitations have already gone out," was my attempt to sway the conversation to my contemporary view on marriage.

"Forget the invitations," she said. "That's just paper . . . I'm talking *life.*"

So began my mother-daughter talk shortly after I had consented to marry Denzel. He wasn't the famous Denzel Washington at that point. If anything, my career was the one that was booming. At that time I had quite a name for myself as a classical pianist and a Broadway performer.

"A good woman can make a bad man good, and a bad woman

can make a good man bad," continued Mom on her philosophy of marriage. "It's all about influence. That's your power as a woman.

"God created us—the woman—as a helpmate. We have a responsibility as a helpmate to recognize our power and to use our power for the good of the kingdom."

Mom looked at me to make sure I was still paying close attention.

"The original design of marriage is of God, and the wife has a very strong role in this design. Now, can you do this?" she asked.

I didn't know at the time because I was still a bit stuck on the "85 percent," so I was resisting. I felt it to be *so* unfair. How could this be?

As I pondered the unfairness I felt about her theory, I had to examine my mother's role as I saw it in her own marriage . . . as it affected our family. I then had to admit that my parents' marriage was one of total unity. They were truly *one*. Teamwork personified! There was never an issue as to what was the role of the woman or the role of the man. It was just whoever was available to do the job at hand, did it.

So I asked, "How do I do it?"

"Not at all by yourself," said Mom. "You must be guided 100 percent by God, totally giving your marriage to Him. Then, you and Denzel must pray. The two of you must pray together. *Constantly!*"

I can still see the passion in her face as she continued to give me her blueprint for a successful marriage.

Prayer, hmmm . . . I thought.

Then with that gentle, beautiful smile of hers, she left me to think about it all.

I then prayed. After my prayer, I felt confident that I could do the 85 percent. I felt confident because I knew that prayer worked for *everything*!

I had been a part of a praying family. My siblings and I knew the power of prayer because we witnessed it, to the point that it was an integral part of our lives. I had grown up with prayer as a regular part of our household; therefore, it would not be anything out of the ordinary for me to pray.

I saw Mom and Dad pray together and remember thinking how romantic it seemed, that the two of them were so much closer when I saw them pray together.

They made my brother, sister, and me pray together.

Given all these memories, I said, "*Yes*, I *can* do this!"

Having God at the center of our relationship, Denzel and I have been blessed with twenty-five married years together.

Forget About 50/50

As Pauletta's mother stated, there should be no thinking about 50/50. While she suggested 85/85, we'll even audaciously propose 100/100.

Each partner should plan to put in 100 percent. After all, if you told your boss you were going to put in 50 percent versus the company's 50 percent, what do you suppose the response would be?

As a quick thinker, you'd probably pledge to put in 110 percent . . . making our suggestion of a mere 100 percent quite reasonable, right?

PRAYER AND COMMUNICATION

Once your and your spouse's minds are focused on total commitment in your marriage, let's add the element of daily prayer.

When we engage in the daily habit of prayer, an extraordinary realm of communication begins to emerge The action of speaking to God as a single, committed force naturally invokes an aura of reverence, making it less conducive to scorekeeping and griping. We find that there is almost an unwritten rule that prayer is no time to reflect upon your partner's shortcomings or unveil a laundry list of things you want God to change in your partner.

Joint prayer should begin with an expression of gratitude to God for all of the positive things He has provided you. Prayer is when we need to ask for guidance from above on our own shortcomings and needs, while expressing concerns for the well-being of our families.

When you and your partner arrive at a genuine comfort level in your daily conversations with God, which will occur more rapidly than you'd imagine, you will find yourselves in a phenomenal new realm—a level of communication with the love of your life that takes you into a deep sense of intimacy.

Jazz singer Bill Cantos says, "When you are with God, you're as honest and unguarded as you ever get."

His wife Mari adds: "While praying together, the woman sees the heart of the man. I see what Bill is obsessing about . . . what's on his mind. I understand if he's more preoccupied with financial matters, or if he's more concerned about the release of his new CD than I thought. I see his heart and respect him more."

21

> STUDIES SHOW THAT MARRIED
> COUPLES SPEND LESS THAN A HALF-HOUR A
> WEEK TALKING TO EACH OTHER.[1]
>
> —DEBORAH TANNEN, PH.D.

COMMUNICATION: WOMEN VERSUS MEN

It is a popular belief that the number one need of women in marriage is frequent, meaningful communication with their husbands.

"Did you know that men generally speak about 2,000 words a day and women 7,000?"[2] That's one way men and women are different. Men focus on goals—something acquired from hunting during caveman days—while women are conditioned to gather information, or so goes playwright Rob Becker's theory in *Defending the Caveman*, Broadway's longest-running nonmusical solo play.[3] He describes a baseball game to help illustrate the point: "[It's] a great man sport . . . because you're out there together focused on a goal and not particularly near to one another. Nodding and spitting convey all the necessary information. But if you let the girls on the field, they collect in the middle and start talking."[4]

Dr. Willard Harley, noted psychologist and author of *His Needs, Her Needs*, says what men want most in a marriage is "sexual fulfillment and recreational companionship" while women tend "to want affection and conversation."[5]

In her book *You Just Don't Understand*, Dr. Deborah Tannen

furthers that thought by describing a man who had a sore arm for several weeks and never bothered mentioning it to his wife. Her feelings were hurt. "Not telling her his arm ached," says Tannen, "meant he was distancing her with his silence."[6]

From the husband's perspective, he was protecting her from worry. He may have thought, *Why should I worry her about my pain since it might be nothing?*

According to Dr. Tannen, men act according to a hierarchical instinct for superiority, exemplified by the games they played as boys; the superior player wins, the other loses. Women, meanwhile, act according to an inbred need for intimacy. Their childhood games include hopscotch and doll-play.

"In her world, imparting of personal information is the fundamental material of intimacy," says Tannen, "so withholding such information deprives her of the closeness that is her life blood." The different interpretation of the same information by a man and a woman reflects that "they are tuned to different frequencies."[7]

You may have read another book published after Dr. Tannen's work, a 1993 bestseller called *Men Are from Mars, Women Are from Venus* by John Gray, which arrived at largely the same conclusion.

So let us agree: as a general rule, women are more inclined to want to talk things over and over while men are inclined to skip the dialogue and get right to the solution. To go slay the dragons.

THE ROLE OF PRAYER IN CONVERSATION

How does prayer affect this genetic distinction between men and women?

Couples who dedicate themselves to daily prayer are finding that by coming before the Almighty, openly discussing matters with Him, the playing field seems to be evened. Women *and* men both tend to enjoy more satisfying and deeper levels of communication in their marriages.

Donna describes this situation when she and her husband, a former police officer who speaks very sparingly, began praying together. "At the beginning of our forty days of prayer, he said little. Then a week or two into it I had to say, 'Hey, Joe. Shut up! Let me have a word or two!'"

Another frequently stated benefit of joint prayer by our test couples is that disagreements were less frequent.

KEY TO FEWER DISAGREEMENTS

"I think we've had fewer disagreements," says Tiffany. "And on those days when we didn't pray, arguments came back."

Tiffany and Matt agree that their daily prayer has contributed to a new tranquility in their marriage; they have fewer disagreements and greater understanding.

Matt explains that prayer has helped him to express himself. "I grew up in the city, where you don't wear your feelings on your sleeve because people take advantage of you," he admits, noting that during prayer there is a feeling of safety; he can be unreserved in opening up to God.

"It's amazing how much God has softened his heart," says Tiffany. "The rough-and-tumble city boy who liked to fight now wells up while watching *Extreme Makeover: Home Edition*," a popular TV series that tugs at the heartstrings.

Daily Prayer and the Daily Grind

"I'm trying to think—gosh, what did we do before we prayed together?" says Shellie, a gregarious and energetic suburban mother and wife who balances life with the dexterity of a juggler.

Shellie and Dan decided to take The 40 Day Prayer Challenge even though joint prayer had long been a part of their twenty-one years of marriage.

"Two months ago I would have said, 'Oh, we pray every day.' But you don't realize there are days when something happens, and you skip. You don't mean to, you don't think about it," says Shellie.

As it turned out, their commitment to pray together a minimum of five minutes a day for forty days occurred at a time when their family faced multiple uncertainties.

Shellie recounts the feelings of being overwhelmed. "We had so many challenges . . . our daughter's mysterious illness, our son's wedding, the move from one city to another . . . we were sitting on the edge of our chair saying, 'Okay God, if You don't handle this, it can't get handled.' But I think we both felt empowered by His Holy Spirit to handle everything."

Dan notes the importance of placing a priority on praying together. "Sometimes we get lax. The day starts, we're off and running, and somewhere down the day we say, 'Oh, man, we blew it.'"

What were the signs that they "blew it"?

"Crabbiness," says Dan, explaining that on days when he and Shellie pray together, there is less friction and more harmony.

A banker by profession, Dan could see another advantage to taking The 40 Day Prayer Challenge. "The best thing was we were made accountable. We said we'd do it, and we needed to fulfill that commitment."

Shellie is grateful that simultaneous to completing their forty-day pledge, they successfully emerged from their season of stressfulness.

"Praying moved the hand of God," she sighs with relief.

Then glancing at her husband, she smiles playfully. "But it also really ignited something in us too. Boy . . . to have those moments where it feels like you are on your honeymoon again was great."

TWO FIRECRACKERS READY TO EXPLODE

"We were a rebellious couple—unprepared for life, much less matrimony," says Patsy Clairmont.

Today, the five-foot bundle of energy with spiked hair is on tour as a leading international speaker, including the popular Women of Faith® circuit to nearly thirty cities, captivating annual audiences of more than 400,000 attendees.

Patsy was seventeen and Les was eighteen when she became a teenage bride. "I was a runaway, a high school dropout, and Les was in and out of trouble."

She describes her husband as barrel-chested and five foot nine and a half—gigantic, compared to her petite stature.

"His explosive anger scared me," she confesses. "Les came from a volatile home; he didn't want to emulate that, but he couldn't help it. As a result, we both became verbally abusive with each other."

Patsy said the constant anxiety in their young marriage contributed to her becoming agoraphobic, the fear of leaving her home . . . even going to the store.

Desperate to find solutions, Patsy turned to God.

"I kept thinking that the Lord would fix me and our marriage," she says softly. Yet even though Les came to Christ a year or two after her, their disagreements and verbal assaults continued unabated.

Patsy felt desperate—stuck in a place with no way out. Then there was a divine intervention.

"In the midst of yet another argument, not knowing what else I could do, I dropped to my knees and cried out for God to enter into our terrible situation, to rescue us, to bring us peace."

Les was stunned by his wife's action.

"So was I," says Patsy. "Les turned and left the house. But when he came back a short while later, we sat down, prayed, and talked things out."

That was the first time as a couple that either of them experienced the power of prayer to help them "step through to the other side of a squabble."

"At that moment of resolve and forgiveness, a healing change began in our marriage," says Patsy. "When my husband saw the potential of resolving conflict through prayer, he entered into it quickly. He was the first to initiate prayer . . . wrapping me in his arms . . . and praying for Christ's love over me."

After that life-changing day, Patsy and Les incorporated daily prayer into their lives, whenever and however they could. She travels thousands of miles to conferences nationally and internationally, but says, "It is not unusual for us to pray over the phone."

Today, Pasty and Les are madly in love and have celebrated forty-five years of marriage.

"We've learned how prayer changes our attitude . . . getting us past our humanity to hear each other's heart."

TO THE MOON, ROBIN

Dave's problem was self-control. He knew it. He could feel it coming on. Something would set him off, and inner anger would rise up, out of control, like an overflowing toilet basin, then explode as an errant rocket in the direction of his most convenient dumping ground: Robin, his wife.

It was actually a beautiful weekend. After six months of foster parenting, little Katie had been tearfully returned to her family, providing Robin and Dave with their first romantic getaway in months: Niagara Falls, on the Canadian side, where a casino hotel had views of the falls.

It had also been four weeks since Dave's surgery left him hobbling with an aluminum walker, in considerable pain, and with one foot devoid of feelings. He fretted that he'd lose his hard-won placement with a local band, and never again be able to use that foot to strike the bass drum pedal.

It was into the night of their second day. Dave and Robin were bubbly and chatty, waiting in line to convert their Canadian winnings to American. Dave had not only hit the slot machine jackpot for two thousand nickels, but he'd also been victorious in a basketball wagering game. Absentmindedly summing up their wonderful weekend, they handed the woman behind the window about $190 in estimated winnings.

"Coming here was probably the best thing we could have done," said Dave, leaving unspoken the sadness they both felt after giving up the foster child.

"I know," smiled Robin. "And we're leaving with more money than we started with."

Robin was handed a small stack of American bills. Both glanced at it briefly, continuing the conversation as they walked away. Puzzlement simultaneously crossed their minds, wondering how the exchange rate could produce such a small stack of bills. Robin spoke first.

"Wait. This can't be right. There's . . ." quickly counting the money in her hand, "only $75 here. We gave her almost $200."

"Did you drop any of it?" asked Dave, faintly recalling that Robin had dropped a bill earlier in the day. He sounded a bit too accusatory.

"No. I did not drop any of it," retorted Robin defensively, befuddled herself by what could have happened.

"There's no way that woman could have made a mistake," charged Dave. "This is their business . . . counting money all day long." His blood pressure was starting to rise with the judgment that if it wasn't the casino's fault, it surely must be Robin's.

"Are you sure you didn't spend some of that money?" rejoined Robin, employing the knee-jerk tactic that the best defense is any old defense. Moreover, Dave had a habit of throwing good money after bad when he was losing, hoping against hope he'd recoup. Perhaps he'd done that again.

"No," he said, loud enough to turn the heads of passersby, "I stuck to our agreement when we came in here: just spending what we planned to spend. No more."

"Are you sure?" scowled Robin.

"I can't believe you're accusing me of stealing the money!" shouted Dave, blood now testing the boiling point.

"I'm not accusing you of stealing . . . but in the past . . ."

"Well, I didn't steal it . . . I didn't spend it . . . and if you didn't lose it, where could it be?" His mind swiftly searched for someone else to blame. "You know what? That lady saw us talking, not paying attention. She scammed us. This is a scam!"

"Calm down. I'm going back to talk with her," Robin appeased.

"What? Are you kidding? You're gonna tell me you're going to go to the window and tell that woman she gave you the wrong amount of money? You're outta your mind. What do you think she's going to say? 'Oh, you're right, dear . . . I made a mistake. Here. Here's a handful of cash to replace it.'"

"Do you need to be talking so loud?"

"What does it matter? It's a scam. We've had it. We're done. Put a fork in us, we're *done!*"

Robin departed for the window, again taking up a place in line while Dave, his clanking walker accentuating his festering temper, retreated to a nearby sitting (and sulking) area.

At the window the woman patiently listened to Robin's plea that she'd cashed in nearly $200 Canadian and had only $75 American to show for it. The woman glanced at the clock and said the only way she'd know if a mistake had happened was if she discovered an overage in her drawer when she cashed out. That was a half hour from then.

Robin sighed, and determined she'd wait, shifting to one side of the window.

At a distance, Dave was simmering again. He concluded that nothing good was coming from Robin's visit with the cashier.

This was a waste of time. And surely they must be stiffing her . . . giving her the runaround . . . trying to cover up their scam!

Pulling himself to his feet, Dave angrily grabbed the aluminum walker and began his slow march to the window to see what was going on. *Clank. Clank. Clank.*

Robin tried her best to explain to her impatient husband what procedures needed to be followed before a mistake could be confirmed.

"Say good-bye to your money, Robin. That woman's got it in her shoe."

Clank. Clank. Clank. He clanked back to his seat.

The next half hour passed slowly. The woman cashed out her American money drawer and reported that everything was in order. Only by waiting a while longer would they be able to determine the outcome of the Canadian drawer.

At nearly 12:45 a.m., Dave could see the woman huddling with coworkers in animated conversation. Curiosity got the best of him. This time his approach to Robin, still waiting near the window, was noiseless.

The woman motioned for Robin to step forward.

"Well . . . it looks like I'm $100 over in Canadian," said the woman apologetically. "I'll have to recount it to be sure. It'll just be a few minutes more."

Robin looked blankly at Dave.

Assuming the sad, hound-dog face of Jackie Gleason as Ralph Kramden in *The Honeymooners*, Dave softly whimpered, "Aw honey, I did it again. I flew off the handle. I ruined this whole weekend. I'm sorry."

"I accept your 'sorry,'" said Robin unemotionally.

"No, I can tell by your look, you're not accepting it," said Dave, then catching himself backsliding into anger, he quickly mimicked Gleason with Ralph Kramden's famous line: "One of these days, Alice . . . bang, zoom, right to the moon!"

"Ahem . . ." said the woman at the window. "Here you go. Thanks for your patience." She handed Robin the American equivalent of one hundred Canadian dollars.

Walking away, Dave was not quite ready to look at the glass half full. "Here we were planning to go to bed early tonight. You know, by rights, they should give us something for our time."

Ignoring his comment, Robin accentuated the positive. Proud of her accomplishment, flashing a big smile, she said, "Hey. We got our money back!"

Dave, suddenly captivated by her loving smile and enthusiasm, reverted to his version of Jackie Gleason's barreling voice. "Baby, you're the greatest!"

With Robin holding Dave by the arm, they clanked away.

How did Robin and Dave's participation in The 40 Day Prayer Challenge—praying together daily—affect behavior? To begin with, they decided to forego any further casino visits. As for Dave's tendency to involuntarily explode and reenact a scene from *The Honeymooners*, let's find out. The following conversation occurred just after they had finished The 40 Day Prayer Challenge.

Q&A WITH ROBIN AND DAVE

Q: *Was there a pattern to your flying off the handle?*

Dave: No, Ralph Kramden would come out for no rhyme or

reason. But I have to admit, since we've been doing our forty days, he hasn't been out at all.

Robin: We're more conscious of automatically reacting with hostility in a situation like that.

Dave: We might have words, but now, in the heat of the moment, we sit down and discuss it rationally.

Robin: Dave is the one likely to say, "Let's stop and pray." I'm the one who wants to be mad. But I take my cues from his willingness to pray.

Dave: A lot of our disagreements were about my health situation. I know Robin was frustrated because she couldn't do anything to help me.

Robin: When there's a disagreement, it's usually not about the issue itself, but how we belabored it. Nothing lasts a long time now . . . we respect each other more and because we are likely to stop and pray, things are less likely to get out of control.

Dave: I agree with that. It's hard to be mad when you're praying.

S.T.O.P.

Sometimes it's helpful to have a mental-conditioning device to help you stop yourself from getting into an argument in the first place. Dave and Robin tried this and it's helped them.

We call it S.T.O.P.

The next time you're about to fly off the handle like Ralph Kramden, do this:

S—*shhhhh*   Quiet yourself.

T—*think*   Before you utter your next words, *consciously* think rather than placing yourself on autoverbal regurgitation.

O—*organize*   Take this moment—organize what you are going to say.

P—*pray*   In this split second, you need to pray for the protection of your marriage.

Few things wound your partner more deeply than how you speak to him or her. Speak with love and respect.

HEAT IN THE KITCHEN

"If I was upset, he would be more upset," says Anqunette, the attractive news anchorwoman. "But the prayer challenge helped us to diffuse those situations."

Her husband, Dan, agrees. As a chef-manager, he would sometimes "feel the heat in the kitchen" in more ways than one; the objective was to not bring it home with him.

"We were both going through some career-related stress during the forty days," he says, "but I noticed, after praying together, our anxiety levels were not as high. In fact, overall, disagreements were less."

At the outset of their prayer time together, Anqunette was more hesitant. "I think I was more introverted than Dan," she admits. "I felt praying together was very private."

But now that they've ventured into the sanctity of the most

intimate act between a man and a woman, they've determined that joint prayer is not something they are going to stop.

No Fight Zone

"We haven't had an argument in twenty-seven years!"

You may be thinking: *That can't be possible. How could two people be married for nearly three decades and never have an argument?*

Michael and Ethel Patrick assured us they weren't fibbing. They've simply never argued. Here's how. Each has appreciated that there are times when they've had differences of opinion, but, in every case, they sought solutions with amicable attitudes.

"When Ethel and I differ on any situation," says Michael, "we discuss the problem, looking at all the pros and cons."

They begin with the premise that they are on the same team. And that means they are in accord on finding the best possible outcome, not on who *wins*.

"If Ethel is passionate about something, I listen," continues Michael. "I try to understand her point of view. Then we bring the problem into our daily prayer time and allow God to become our mediator."

"If you think back upon an argument" says Ethel, "does anyone win when you lose your cool?"

Listen to your partner, ask questions, and try to walk in his shoes or see her side of it. Then discuss your differences. Finally, pray about it. You'll find that the decision you make with God's input and your joint desire for accord will benefit you both.

> ## LOVE NEVER FAILS.
>
> —1 CORINTHIANS 13:8 NKJV

I Don't Feel Like Talking with You, God

"I'm mad at You right at this moment, God. I don't feel like talking with You today; what's the point? Are You even hearing me?"

With wry Italian humor, former supermodel Cristina Ferrare discloses that her prayer relationship with the Almighty is very emotional.

"I go through these prideful periods when I think I don't really need God; then when I do, I feel my problems are so selfish and unworthy of God's time . . . I don't know what I should do."

Cristina decided to take up the challenge of praying with her husband, Tony, to see if that would work better for her.

"I had heard about the power of praying as a couple and wondered about what I had always believed . . . that where two or three are gathered in His name, He is there in the midst," referring to a favorite Bible verse.[8]

Cristina and Tony decided to take The 40 Day Prayer Challenge.

The popular television talk-show host shifted the conversation, reflecting upon the spiritual journey of her twenty-three-year marriage to Tony Thomopoulos, studio executive and former ABC Entertainment president. She elaborated on how she and Tony had worked at melding their distinct religious backgrounds into a strong harmonious unit of faith.

"We grew together and found a church that was comfortable and that we could relate to. Slowly we started our walk of faith together. Today, Tony is so far ahead of me that I can't keep up with him! He is definitely the spiritual head of the family—and a great inspiration."

Yet prior to taking The 40 Day Prayer Challenge, Cristina and Tony had never prayed together as a couple, other than table grace or at church.

"It was a journey we'd not taken before," says Tony. "But I have to tell you . . . it's very satisfying."

"The reason it took us so long," says Cristina, "is I was too embarrassed to pray about things out loud and expose my innermost feelings. I thought if I did, Tony would think less of me. It is an intimate act, and it involves a lot of trust on both sides. It took courage to be so open and to feel you're not being judged."

Tony smiles agreeably. "It was easier for me to expose my inner feelings during prayer."

Cristina continues: "I said to Tony, 'We have to make this commitment every single night. You and I must take the time to pray together.' We started doing just that, and things have started to change in our family, our relationship, and our businesses."

But the charismatic television performer was not yet finished displaying her disarming trademark . . . delightful outspokenness.

"The other night Tony and I had a huge argument before we went to bed. I was really mad at him. I told him, 'You know what? I'm not going to pray with you tonight.'

"He left the room in a huff and annoyed.

"He came back a few minutes later—he took my hand and said very calmly, 'Let's say our prayers.' So we did. I don't even remember what we fought about."

Cristina pauses, momentarily pensive.

"I wake up every morning to the most exquisite view of the morning sky and green rolling hills. My first thought is always of God. How could it not be? The reminder of His great presence and love is right outside my window. I reach for Tony's hand, and we begin our day as a couple who pray."

COMMUNICATION MIGHT BE CONTAGIOUS

Jeff and Janice found that when they maintained joint daily prayer, there were fewer disagreements, but also there was an inducement for more-extended communication between the two of them.

"One week we didn't pray regularly because Janice was traveling," observes Jeff, "and we found we were short with each other more often."

Married twenty-seven years, Jeff and Janice were churchgoing Christians who said grace at dinnertime. But prior to taking The 40 Day Prayer Challenge, they had no discipline of praying together every day. Moreover, without realizing it, they'd developed patterns of less-frequent communication.

"We'd gotten into a habit of watching TV during dinner. But when we started joint prayer, we established a new routine: turning off the TV and talking. After dinner we move to the living room, read scripture, and pray," says Janice.

"Then we just sit and talk," adds Jeff.

Janice laughs as a humorous experience comes to mind. "One evening we talked and talked for about an hour and a half until we realized, 'Hey, we've been sitting here in the dark.'"

They both laugh.

"It was totally dark, and we hadn't even noticed it," chuckles Jeff.

Praying together is a habit Jeff and Janice have no intention of abandoning. "It's as important as taking a shower or going to work every day," says Jeff, looking to his wife with accord.

"It's a part of our lives," smiles Janice.

"We're going to keep doing this for the rest of our lives," they say in unison.

RESEARCH ON COMMUNICATION

Although it is generally accepted that frequent communication is vital for a successful relationship, the Gallup studies showed that even in marriages where conversation was less frequent but where couples were in the habit of frequent prayer, chances for divorce were greatly lowered.

"Joint prayer seems to be an effective substitute for conversation . . . the family that prays together, it has been argued, stays together,"[9] writes Andrew Greeley.

SECTION

TAKING THE 40 DAY
PRAYER CHALLENGE

THE 40 DAY PRAYER CHALLENGE™

All right.

Do you have the proper mind-set to begin exploring this extraordinary manner of renovating your marriage?

Are you both ready to make the commitment to giving joint daily prayer a chance to work wonders in your relationship? To help you work through issues that have been bothering you . . . bringing you tangible things you need . . . while vastly enhancing your love life and communication?

Can the two of you mutually agree to pray for as little as five minutes a day—even by telephone if you're unable to be together— for a forty-day test?

That's all it takes.

ESTABLISHING A HABIT

There's a popular notion that establishing a habit takes about twenty days—three weeks, roughly. That includes establishing a *good* habit like daily exercise. Or breaking a *bad* habit like smoking.

We believe that if you, as a couple, put your minds to the importance of praying together for twenty days, you'll be into the rhythm of it. And by committing for an additional three weeks, a total of forty days, *you will own the new habit.*

By the time you have completed your first twenty days of praying together you'll have developed your own style, adapting your prayer habit into the unique pattern of your own lives—including where you pray, when you pray, and for how long.

WHY FORTY DAYS?

A six-week period is not only a good time period to establish the habit of praying together, but the dedication of forty days also has biblical significance.

"Whenever God wanted to prepare someone for his purposes, he took forty days," says Rick Warren, author of the all-time best-selling *The Purpose Driven Life*.[1] Warren points to these examples:

- Noah's life was transformed by forty days of rain.
- Moses was transformed by forty days on Mount Sinai.
- David was transformed by Goliath's forty-day challenge.
- Jesus was empowered by forty days in the wilderness.
- The disciples were transformed by forty days with Jesus, following His resurrection.

Your marriage can be transformed by forty days of praying together!

Think about that. The most important factor for peace and happiness in your life can be totally transformed in forty days.

This will be a life-changing experience. And if you keep to your commitment, you simply will not believe the outcome. That's a promise.

THE MECHANICS OF THE 40 DAY PRAYER CHALLENGE™

In the next chapter, we help you through the most frequently asked question: "How do we do it?"—meaning, how do you get started, where is it best to pray, and what are the guidelines?

But for now, let us reveal the procedures of The 40 Day Prayer Challenge.

First, we ask you to individually fill out the questionnaire found at the back of this book or online as described on the next page. The word *individually* is important. We're all tempted to do our kids' homework for them. And there may be a tendency for one of the two of you to say, "Oh, he or she is too busy right now . . . I'll fill it out."

That won't serve you well.

You *both* need to sit down together and answer the brief questions.

The questionnaire has been crafted with the guidance of the Institute for Studies of Religion at Baylor University. Our primary purpose is to help you identify factors about your relationship and give you benchmarks of your progress. At the end of the forty days, we ask that you fill out an exit questionnaire, which will give you a way in which to measure many of the demarcations of improvements in your relationship.

To fill out the questionnaire online, log on to www.coupleswho pray.com. The online questions formulated by Baylor University are a bit more extensive, and all tabulations for your initial and exit responses are calculated at the Institute for Studies of Religion.

If you sign up for The 40 Day Prayer Challenge online, you will receive an ongoing system of support. We will send weekly e-mails to you with short stories and other tips we have put together to encourage you along your forty-day journey.

The coupleswhopray.com Web site also serves as a resource hub, providing you access to video presentations, CWP journals, and other helpful information while offering links to marital support services.

The online execution of the questionnaire will allow you to guage your progress from the start to the end of your forty-day experience—everything from how often you and your partner talk with each other to how frequently you hold hands. As well, you will be able to compare your end results with others in a national average.

Either way, it's your choice. And in either case, it's anonymous.

Let's begin. Please look over and fill out the initial questionnaire in appendix 1, or log on to www.coupleswhopray.com and fill out the one there.

WHY THE 40 DAY PRAYER CHALLENGE™ WORKS

Nearly all couples in our pilot group who committed themselves to taking The 40 Day Prayer Challenge became genuinely excited about the results they began seeing in their marriages after only two or three weeks.

Nearly every couple continued to pray together for a minimum of five minutes a day, even when travel schedules and other family obligations hindered them. "It was worth it, to somehow find that precious five minutes between me and my husband and God . . . whether it was by phone or before we got out of bed," said one woman.

And nearly every couple who participated in the forty-day test said they wouldn't give it up for anything.

Still, you may be saying, "Yeah, but . . . I still don't understand how you do it."

That's the next chapter.

HOW DO YOU DO IT?

The man behind the wheel glanced at us.

"Your comment last night really got me thinking . . . when you said that prayer was the 'most intimate act between a man and a woman.'"

We nodded appreciatively.

We were being driven to the airport by a tall, stocky off-duty member of the Oklahoma City police force, who was also a member of the megachurch where we had spoken the night before on the principles in this book.

"But how do you do it?" he asked disarmingly.

We looked at each other.

"I mean, my wife and I pray. She prays separately, and I pray separately, but how do we do it together?"

That innocent, childlike question from a burly cop led us to understand that many of you might be asking the same question.

Even if you both pray—separately—the idea of coming together to participate in the most intimate act anyone can imagine may seem as though we are asking you to cross the Verazzano-Narrows Bridge—the longest suspension bridge in the United States—on your hands and knees.

Yet couple after couple has shown that it only takes one of you to grasp your partner's hand and say, "Honey, would you mind sitting with me while we pray? You don't even have to say a thing."

You'll soon turn that long, long bridge into a mere footpath.

Here are ten thoughts to get you going.

TEN TIPS TO START THE 40 DAY PRAYER CHALLENGE™

1. More prayer, more power!

Prayer is simply talking with God. He invites you to come into His presence so He can love, encourage, and teach you. God also wants to help the two of you build a marital foundation that is lasting and unshakable, with Him in the middle. Therefore, the more you pray, the more power will come to you.

2. Make time to pray.

Find a mutual time conducive to establishing your routine of praying. Is it easier in the morning or at night? Some couples find it better to get up a few minutes early before the kids. Some find it more suitable before bedtime. If you're apart, pray on the phone.

3. Have an attitude of gratitude and vulnerability.
Recall things God has done for you, individually and as a couple. Thank Him for specific blessings: your children, your health, your home, and your income. And go ahead—be vulnerable. After all, you're talking with God. He knows everything about you anyway!

4. Confess and request forgiveness.
Honestly ask God to show you where your problem areas are, freely confessing those problems you perceive. He wants to free you from the shackles of resentfulness, insecurity, mistrust, doubt, guilt, shame, fear, uncertainty. Don't own it anymore. Give it all to Him. Let God carry your baggage.

5. Pray out loud with your spouse.
At the outset, perhaps only one of you will speak. But as you become more comfortable, both of you will want to state your concerns and requests. Praying is like exercise . . . the more you do it, the more natural it becomes. And the more indispensable it is in your life.

6. Keep it short.
Prayers don't need to be long-winded or flowery. If you each speak for one or two minutes, that's just fine. As you develop your own style and patterns, you may find yourself extending the experience.

7. Use everyday language.
God does not require *thee*'s and *thou*'s. Imagine that you are sitting down to have an open, intimate conversation with a father with

whom you are completely at ease, who lovingly listens to every word and wants to give you anything you ask for. It's your heart—not your tongue—from which He wants to hear.

8. Pray for your marriage.

Your intimate prayer sessions must never be a time for bringing up your partner's shortcomings. In fact, this is when you need to be the most sensitive to each other's feelings. Focus on *us*. Use kind and encouraging words about each other. Thank God for your spouse. Ask Him to show you ways in which you can love and support each other more. As you pray together, you will become more and more united in your thoughts and desires.

9. Pray for others and for self.

Praying for family and others is what many people have learned is the only way to pray. That is important. But God also desires that you ask His help for yourself too. Ask, believe, and receive is the biblical command for you to *believe* that you will *receive* what you've *asked* for (see Matthew 21:21–22; Mark 11:23–24). Except those things He would not be pleased with, nothing is off-limits. He wants you to cast *all* of your cares upon Him.

10. Expect God to answer your prayers.

Pray with the expectation that God hears and is answering your prayers. Thank Him for your blessings even before He gives them to you. The manifestation of prayer may not be seen right away, but trust that He always hears and answers requests. Perhaps not in the way you think or on your timetable. But as you continue to mentally and physically strive to claim your requests, God is working. It's in the waiting that God does the work. And in the waiting He's building your faith. As promised: "Faith is the substance of things hoped for, the evidence of things not seen" (Heb. 11:1 KJV).

IT'S NOT WHERE YOU START . . . BUT WHERE YOU FINISH

"Frank and I both believe very much in the power of prayer, we just tend to approach it differently," says Kathie Lee Gifford with a smile and gusto.

For fifteen years, Kathie Lee's upbeat personality lit up living-room TVs in the mornings. And for twenty-seven years, Frank Gifford's smooth style lent personality and expertise to ABC's *Monday Night Football,* based upon his stature as one of the greatest players of all time.

Kathie Lee and Frank are among the nation's most talked-about, speculated-about, fascinated-about media personalities. In fact, you may wonder what an incredible nuisance it must be to find yourself the subject of stalking paparazzi or constantly to be taken out of context by those whose livelihood is picking apart the private lives of others.

But Kathie Lee and Frank Gifford are well grounded in their faith, with priorities firmly planted: God, marriage, children, and family. Protecting those priorities was at the root of Kathie Lee's decision to leave morning television in 2000. And whenever the Giffords are targeted for attention, it's the fortress of their faith that shields them.

But how are they different in their prayer?

"I can't help but think God is really busy," says Frank with a smile. "I try to understand the speed of light and the concept of no end to the universe and I'm very grateful to be here. I think, *What an awesome God*."

Kathie Lee extends the thought. "Frank's attitude is, *How could I possibly ask God for more than He has already given me?* But asking God seems totally right to me because it's based on Scripture. 'Ask and you shall be given, seek and you shall find, knock and it shall be opened unto you.'"

"Kathie Lee is about the moment," adds Frank, "while I try to understand infinity, those things for which there is no explanation. Hers is an intimate relationship with God. Mine is vast."

The couple's appreciation for the goodness of God is rooted in their upbringing.

"My family was very spiritual," says Frank. "They'd take me to the huge Los Angeles temple of Aimee Semple McPherson," describing a phenomenally popular evangelist of the era. "I was influenced about the power of God right from the beginning."

"People think Frank was born with a silver spoon in his mouth," adds Kathie Lee. "He didn't have a spoon. He grew up poverty-stricken . . . ate dog food sometimes. And I barely had a spoon, but it was plastic. So both of us grew up with very little. At least my father had a job. His father was an oil worker. Frank lived in forty-seven different places before he was in high school because his father was constantly looking for the next oil job. And that was during the Depression. We know what struggle is."

Casting an appreciative glance around her, Kathie Lee brought her story to present time. "Frank and I are in a position where we cannot believe that we now live with such incredible bounty. But we both know that 'to whom much is given, much is required,'" she says, quoting another favorite verse. "We both have a tremendous feeling of the responsibility of that."

Returning to their distinctions in prayer, Kathie Lee says thoughtfully, "Frank's sort of a pragmatist."

Then with a tone that predicts a punch line, she adds, "But we've found the way to pray together, by letting him do the thanking and letting me do the asking!"

Frank rejoins, "It's not about the content but the connection."

Paraphrasing the Broadway song, "It's Not Where You Start, But Where You Finish," Kathie Lee joyfully proclaims, "We may not start together . . . but we sure end together!"

One wonders if the harmony of Kathie Lee and Frank's marriage began with the godwink of their identical birth dates. They both were born on August 16.

Differences

If God made every grain of sand unique, then we shouldn't be surprised that He made each of us different. No two of us are alike and no two pray alike. God is in all things, from the vastness of the universe to the smallest hummingbird. He cares about every big thing and every little thing in our lives.

Like Frank, let's appreciate God's awesome creation. And as with Kathie Lee, let us appreciate His attention to detail.

Celebrate the joy in your distinctions.

CHECK YOUR BAGGAGE

We all have baggage. It's inescapable. Some have more than others.

Here's a fact about baggage: you simply cannot change what's happened in the past. Period. But you can *choose* to live in the present, leaving the past where it belongs. Behind.

If you continue to drag your baggage—or worse, someone else's baggage—all through life with you, it'll only serve to pull you down and never stop haunting your relationships with those you love.

Here's another fact: your baggage is not going away on its own. You need a *baggage handler* to dispose of it—to put it in its proper place.

Your redcap is God. He created you to be free of your past.

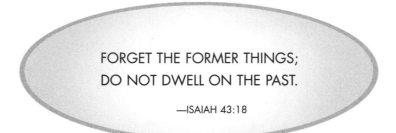

FORGET THE FORMER THINGS;
DO NOT DWELL ON THE PAST.

—ISAIAH 43:18

MAMA . . . IS THAT YOU FOLLOWING ME?

Robert was fifty years old and never married. He had the desire to get married, and wanted a wife he could grow old with—someone who'd be his best friend and confidante.

He dated many wonderful women, but when the time came

to take the plunge, he always convinced himself that they just didn't measure up. He'd get to that crucial point in the relationship . . . then sabotage it.

Robert finally found a woman who had more potential than all the others. He loved her. He told himself that just maybe it was okay to make the ultimate commitment. *After all*, he reasoned, *I'm getting older, and time is running out.*

After three years of dating, he still hadn't proposed.

He and his girlfriend decided to seek counseling.

The core of the problem was the fact that Robert's mother had been married and divorced several times and he was frozen in a fear of failing at marriage.

He was holding on to the notion that if his mom couldn't stay married, then he'd probably inherited the same problem.[1]

Robert was looking through a lens clouded with *his mother's past choices*. He was carrying *her* baggage.

What a shame. He wasted all those years of companionship because he was dragging around baggage that didn't even belong to him.

He wanted complete assurance his marriage wouldn't fail. A contract. With a guarantee, perhaps.

Well, we all have a contract . . . with our best baggage handler.

CLEAN YOUR WINDSHIELD

As you move forward in The 40 Day Prayer Challenge, please consider starting with a new perspective, looking at the world ahead through your windshield—not your rearview mirror.

Don't let your past dictate where you're going. Your past is yesterday. You can't change it. Learn from it, and move on.

Will Rogers once advised, "Don't let yesterday use too much of today."

So leave your baggage where it belongs.

Beside the road.

> GOD, GIVE US GRACE TO ACCEPT
> WITH SERENITY THE THINGS THAT CANNOT
> BE CHANGED, COURAGE TO CHANGE THE THINGS
> THAT SHOULD BE CHANGED, AND THE WISDOM
> TO DISTINGUISH THE ONE FROM THE OTHER.[2]
>
> —REINHOLD NIEBUHR

CWP CASE HISTORY—FRED AND ALICE

Married for less than ten years, this was Alice's first marriage and Fred's second.

Alice: I never knew how to pray. My family just didn't believe in God.

Fred: Growing up, we had a housekeeper, Millicent, who taught me prayers. A lot of those prayers stayed with me.

Alice: We pray in bed, usually in the morning or sometimes at night or both.

Fred: It's an intimate place for the intimacy of prayer.

Alice: When we are next to each other praying, I feel that we are in a cocoon of comfort—inside a soft place God has woven just for us—just the three of us: Fred, me, and God. We carry the cocoon with us all during the day, even when we aren't together.

Fred: We pray out loud. And we have physical contact.

Alice: We always hold hands as we pray.

Fred: I think praying together has strengthened our relationship—it's something very personal—it helps us to be more in sync.

Alice: Praying out loud clarifies what's on each other's minds. And because we are asking God for the same things, it puts us on the same page for the day. When I hear what Fred is praying about, it reminds me of things I need to pray about.

My heart is now more and more in love with Fred. Every day I'm falling more in love with him. And every day I think, consciously or unconsciously, *What can I do for Fred?*

Fred: My first marriage was very difficult. My counselor asked me to take a month and at the end of each day to make a judgment, whether this was a good day, a bad day, or a neutral day. At the end of the month, I couldn't fill one hand with good days. But in my marriage to Alice ... every single day is a good day. There's never a bad or neutral day.

Alice: *Commitment* is the wrong word because commitments can be broken. You'd never say you're committed to your children ... they're your life. In the same way, neither is my marriage a commitment ... it's my life.

Fred: I like the word *respect*. We have respect for each other.

Alice: I've found that our joint prayer has become a ritual . . . and rituals are good; they form foundations and stability.

Fred: Arsenio Hall used to say he'd experience the *ahhh* thing. Growing up Jewish, I was taught that prayer was an individual experience. I never thought of it as something you'd share with someone. So when the idea of praying *together* was first suggested, it was the *ahhh* thing for me. It's really wonderful.

JOURNALING: WRITING A DAILY LETTER TO GOD

We'd like you to consider writing a journal as you take your journey through forty days of prayer with your partner. Writing down your thoughts and concerns may not strike you as important. But here's a guarantee: when you look back at your journal several weeks from now and discover how God indeed has spoken to your heart about concerns, or has answered prayers, you'll be amazed.

Our daughter Hilary had been journaling for several years. When moving to a new location she came across some of her earlier journals and sat down to read them. She could hardly believe how many prayers had been answered. She was also struck by how her attitude and prayer life had matured over the years. Her first journal entries were full of desperate prayers for God's help while the more current journals were filled with praise for God's blessings.

Perhaps the idea of journaling seems like something teenage

girls do—keeping a diary—not something for grown adults. A wise elder pastor of a little church in upstate New York once put a different spin on it for us.

"I write a letter to God every day," said Dr. Ralph Lankler.

"What do you write about?" we asked.

"Oh, just anything that's on my mind or tuggin' at my heart," he replied with a sweet smile and twinkling eyes. "It's a letter. So I talk to Him about everything. I thank Him or ask Him to send a little assistance here and there."

If you followed Dr. Lankler's example, you'd begin with a salutation such as "Dear Father" and sign it the same way you'd end a note to your earthly father: "Love . . ."

Keep in mind that your letter or journal doesn't need to be a novel like *War and Peace*; most times, a half or single page is plenty. Just as Dr. Lankler did, talk to God about the things you'd discuss if He were in the room with you, having a cup of coffee and a bagel. Tell Him your concerns. And thank Him for things you've received.

Following is how Tiffany and Matt wrote to God one day in their journal:

What a glorious morning. Matt and I were up at 6:30 and went for a walk. It was foggy, but it was gorgeous to look out over the water, the cranes sitting perfectly still, as if God was painting a beautiful picture to remind us that He is in control. Matt and I prayed as we walked in the morning dew. It really set the day off in a great way. I've noted more joy and contentment in our lives these past days. Thank You, Lord. We love You.

Keeping a journal will help you remember what God has done for you. To underscore that, He advises in the Bible:

> Write, therefore, what you have seen, what is now and what will take place later.
> —Revelation 1:19

HOW TO THINK THOUGHTFULLY

As you journey through The 40 Day Prayer Challenge, think about ways you can express your appreciation to your partner.

Nothing reassures your spouse more than to hear it directly from you that you love him or her, no matter how long you've been married, and that you appreciate the unique qualities that he or she brings to your marriage.

Think about how you can express your appreciation through thoughtfulness.

THE GIFTS

A favorite short story most of us studied in high school ended with these words:

> The magi, as you know, were wise men—wonderfully wise men—who brought gifts to the Babe in the manger . . . But . . . let it be said that of all who give gifts, these two were the wisest.

Of course, it was O. Henry's "The Gift of the Magi," a story that touched many of us deeply and remained in our memories because of the thoughtful love expressed by a young couple who was too poor to buy Christmas gifts.

With Christmas approaching, absent of money, they wrestled with what gift they could possibly give the other to convey how much they meant to each other.

Both had a prized possession.

Jim had a gold watch that was handed down from his father and grandfather. Della had soft beautiful hair flowing from the crown of her head to the back of her knees.

Della decided that the very best gift she could give her husband was a gold chain for his watch. He'd love it. But to get that amount of money would require the sacrifice and the sale of her only object of value: her beautiful hair.

That's what she did. And right after she was shorn, she was gripped with worry.

"Please, God, make him think I am still pretty."

As Jim came home that night, Della stood waiting for him, her head wrapped in a scarf. Eagerly she handed him his gift—the gold watch chain.

Wide-eyed, Della studied her husband's face, anticipating that it would light up with joy.

But the expression on Jim's countenance was astonishment.

For on his way home he'd stopped at a store. He sold his prized gold watch in order to buy Della something she'd longingly studied in a store window. Tortoise-shell combs.

Realizing what each had done, they embraced. The greatest gift of all surged through them . . . the joy of being loved.

"Maybe the hairs on my head are numbered," said Della, paraphrasing a Bible verse, "but nobody could ever count my love for you."

Two Gifts of Thoughtfulness

We are asking you to secretly give your partner two thoughtful gifts before you end The 40 Day Prayer Challenge.

No. We're not recommending you chop off your hair or cash in a family heirloom. Instead, we hope you'll give your spouse two gifts of thoughtfulness that you know he or she will appreciate. Gifts that express *I love you* in a different way than you ever have before.

Here's an example.

We once made a dinner date with a couple we'd known from Boston and who had moved to the West Coast. We arrived at the couple's home in the San Fernando Valley prior to going out to a restaurant. Since we'd arrived slightly early, Carolea invited us into the living room where we sat and chatted for ten or fifteen minutes.

Simultaneously we each heard the arrival of a car in the driveway. Instantly, Carolea jumped up and excused herself.

"This is something I always do," she said, briskly walking to assume a position at the opened front door . . . greeting her husband home.

Later we reflected on that gesture of love . . . a small but meaningful gift of thoughtfulness that Carolea gives her husband every day when he comes home from the office: greeting him at the door.

THE GIFT OF OPINION

"We had this space in our kitchen between the refrigerator and the cabinet that was too small to put anything into, except a place to stick shopping bags," says Robin. "It was a mess."

So one day Robin decided to organize things. At the dollar store she bought several plastic containers with covers that, when stacked atop each other, fit perfectly into the space next to the refrigerator. In one box she put plastic bags, paper items in another, and so on. She placed labels neatly on each container and was proud of herself that her kitchen now looked so much better.

"I hate this," sputtered Dave, searching for the box that contained the plastic bags. As he pulled out one box, the others fell to the floor. The only solution was to take out every box to get to the one he needed.

"I really hate this. Doesn't my opinion count?" he repeated every time he approached the stack of boxes.

"I said, 'Yeah, yeah, yeah,'" admits Robin, "but I also knew that the kitchen was so much neater than before."

During The 40 Day Prayer Challenge, Robin and Dave received a suggestion from us to give their partner a secret gift. Not a gift in a package with a ribbon, but a gift of some little thing that they knew their spouse would appreciate.

Robin thought about Dave's repeated comment, *I hate this*.

Then she thought about her response: *Yeah, yeah, yeah*.

She went shopping. Armed with a tape measure, she found exactly what she wanted at a secondhand shop: a very, very narrow bookcase, six inches across, that fit beautifully into that space next to the refrigerator. Each shelf conveniently held different, easily accessible items. Then she waited for Dave to come home.

"What's this?" said Dave quizzically.

"That's your gift of thoughtfulness," said Robin with the air of game-show hostess Vanna White. Then she explained she realized that she had not valued his opinion. Even if she *said* she did . . . she didn't. So his gift wasn't just bookshelves . . . it was *valuing his opinion*.

"Hey . . . that's great," said Dave, giving her a hug. "I'm really touched."

As with the couple in "The Gift of the Magi," Robin reflects, "It was easy to see how you can give someone you love a gift from the heart."

The greatest gift is not found at a store or under a tree, but in the heart of the one you love.

MY GIFT FOR THE BIRDS— LOUISE'S PERSPECTIVE

I heard banging in the basement several evenings in a row just after SQuire left the dinner table saying he had something to do.

The following weekend I found out what it was all about—it was a wonderful gift.

But let me start at the beginning.

When I was in an earlier marriage and my dad was still alive, he came to stay with us for several weeks in our home outside Los Angeles—a sweet little blue house with white trim and a white picket fence.

Dad was always handy. He could fix things and make things. A carpenter by trade, it seemed that everybody in the neighborhood called on him at one time or another to stop by and fix something. One day I was thrilled to find that he had made a gift for me: a mailbox that replicated my home. Placed on a post, it was a little blue-and-white, cape-style house, complete with a picket fence and a gate. It was the cutest thing. The postman would lift the hinged roof and deposit the mail inside.

All the neighbors loved that mailbox, and soon Dad was replicating each of their houses . . . a string of little matching houses lined the street.

A few years later we moved to another address into a traditional yellow and white colonial home. When Dad came to visit, he was beginning to struggle with failing health. Yet I found him gathering the materials to construct for me another replica of my new house for a mailbox. Unfortunately, Dad never finished it. He became ill and passed away.

One year to the day of my father's funeral, my husband demanded a divorce.

The house was sold and my possessions—including the two mailboxes, relics of happier times—were crated and forgotten.

Several years later, SQuire and I were divinely brought together by the wonderful godwink we discussed in the introduction of this book. After we were married, SQuire and I built our dream home on Martha's Vineyard. I was—and still am—living my dream.

Which brings me to the start of this story. SQuire disappeared into the basement several nights in a row. I had no idea what was going on, but I heard banging.

The following weekend I found out. As a loving gift, my

husband had taken the mailbox houses from the old crate. He repainted the blue and white house and spruced up the picket fence. Then he finished the job Dad was unable to do—putting shingles on the roof of the other little house and painting it yellow and white.

Imagine my surprise when I arrived home from the store that day. At opposite ends of my flower garden, atop six-foot posts, my cute little houses were now birdhouses. By lifting the hinged roofs we could fill the charming little houses with bird food.

An act of love from my dad became a wonderful gift from a loving husband. And the birds couldn't be happier.

We often leave each other secret love notes stuck in a suitcase or propped up in a cupboard. It doesn't take long to execute a loving gesture like that, and small gifts of love can last and last.

Just be inventive. Come up with two gifts of thoughtfulness you can secretly give your partner to show love, without fanfare, just to say, "I love you," before The 40 Day Prayer Challenge ends.

Happiness Versus Joy

All marriages start out striving to create an environment of happiness. Joint prayer will contribute to your success as you continue in that pursuit.

"However, there's a significant difference between happiness and joy," counsels publisher Joey Paul.

Joey and his charming wife, Sharon, have long known that distinction because of reliance on their faith.

"Happiness is a temporary state of contentment," he continues with a smile, "while joy is of the Lord."

He was referencing the wisdom in the Bible that says, "For the joy of the LORD is your strength" (Neh. 8:10).

5

THE REMARKABLE POWER OF PRAYER

It always comes back to this. Is there a God?

How do we know?

When his wife became a believer, Lee Strobel, long a proud atheist, a legal editor for the *Chicago Tribune*, and a Yale Law School graduate, set out to challenge—once and for all—the divinity of Christ and the existence of God Himself.

After exhaustive research, this is what he concluded: "I was once full of confidence that Darwinism justified my atheism. But then ... prompted by the positive changes in my wife ... I began to go beyond the obvious, to set aside my prejudices, to ask questions I had never posed before. I wasn't prepared for what happened . . . the facts of science systematically eroded the foundation of Darwinism until it could no longer support the weight of my atheistic conclusions."

In his book *The Case for a Creator*, Strobel also admits, "I was stunned, yes . . . but I had vowed to follow the facts regardless of the cost—even at the cost of my own smug self-sufficiency."[1]

SCIENCE AND THEOLOGY

Arguments about Darwinism—the belief that man evolved by natural means versus intelligent design, created by God—invariably lead back to the big bang theory. In fact, nearly all scientists now concur that the universe began at one moment in time, about fifteen billion years ago, with one big powerful explosion.

But the intelligent design advocates ask, "Yeah, but who created the big bang?"

Only God could have created something from nothing.

Moreover, they argue, the universe is so perfectly designed that if one planet was out of sync by just a fraction, life on earth could not exist.

Lee Strobel elaborates: "The cosmological constant, which represents the energy density of space, is as precise as throwing a dart from space and hitting a bull's-eye just a trillionth of a trillionth of an inch in diameter on earth."[2]

Thoughts like that are nothing short of astonishing.

ANOTHER PERSPECTIVE

Another man who was an atheist—"and a fairly obnoxious one at that," he adds self-deprecatingly—is one of the nation's most respected scientists: Dr. Francis Collins, heralded by the President of the United States when his team of genetic scientists unveiled the human DNA code.[3]

It has been said that if you were to articulate the catalog of content the geneticists amassed for the three billion codes representing every cell in the body—what Dr. Collins calls the "the instructions for building a human being"—it would take you thirty-one years, day and night, to read it aloud.[4]

It was much earlier in his life when a hospitalized grandmother looked Dr. Collins in the eye and asked, "What do you believe?"[5] That simple, direct question shook him into examining his "willful blindness," a term he learned from *Mere Christianity*, the book by noted scholar and writer C. S. Lewis, to which Dr. Collins turned for answers.

He soon realized "that all of my own constructs against the plausibility of faith were those of a schoolboy" and that C. S. Lewis had himself been an atheist "who had set out to disprove faith on the basis of logical argument." The line of reasoning that rocked his ideas about science and spirit down to their foundation "was right there in the title of Book One: 'Right and Wrong as a Clue to the Meaning of the Universe.'

"The concept of right and wrong appears to be universal among all members of the human species," continues Collins; moreover, "this law appears to apply peculiarly to human beings. Though other animals may at times appear to show glimmerings of a moral sense, they are certainly not widespread."[6]

Dr. Collins expanded upon his conclusions: "A major example of the force we feel from the Moral Law is the altruistic impulse, the voice of conscience calling us to help others even if nothing is received in return."[7]

With moral law as the tipping point, Collins sounded much like Lee Strobel as he confessed, "I had started this journey of intellectual exploration to confirm my atheism . . . now, faith *in* God . . . seemed more rational than disbelief."[8]

But Dr. Collins has chosen not to take a stance of "either science or God." He believes that science *and* God are compatible.

"The consequences of Big Bang theory for theology are profound," he says. "I have to agree. The Big Bang cries out for a divine explanation. It forces the conclusion that nature had a divine beginning. I cannot see how nature could have created itself. Only a supernatural force that is outside of space and time could have done that."[9]

But isn't it interesting that after centuries of extensive celestial study by the most brilliant minds on the planet, from Galileo to Hawking, most of today's scientists—even if they continue to differ on *who* created the big bang—end up pretty much in sync with the explanation of *how* it all began, as was written in the Scriptures three thousand years ago?

> In the beginning God created the heavens and the earth. And God said, "Let there be light," and there was light. Then God said, "Let us make man" . . . male and female he created them.
> —Genesis 1:1, 3, 26–27

WHAT ABOUT PRAYER?

With such scholars as Stroebel and Collins, both prior advocates of atheism—one with a law background, the other medicine—each meticulously deliberating the evidence and ruling in God's favor, let us turn to prayer.

By communicating with God through prayer, what proof is there that He hears us and responds?

Many of us *just know* that God answers our prayers. We've generally arrived at that conclusion through personal experience; at some point in the past we've asked, and we've received.

But you will be pleased to know that other brilliant minds have clinically tested the efficacy of prayer at universities such as Duke, Dartmouth, and Yale.

Dr. Harold Koenig, Duke University's associate professor of medicine and psychiatry, evaluated some twelve hundred studies on the effects of prayers and health as reported in a book he coauthored, *Handbook of Religion and Health*. Following are just some of his findings, implying that people who are religious also communicate to God through prayer:

- Hospitalized people who attended church regularly have an average stay three times shorter than people who don't.
- Heart patients who participated in religion were 14 percent more likely to survive surgery than those who didn't.
- Elderly people who go to church regularly suffered strokes 50 percent less than those who didn't.
- Religious people in Israel were 40 percent less likely to die from cardiovascular disease and cancer than those who were not religious.

And according to Dr. Koenig, "Healthy senior citizens who said they rarely or never prayed ran about a 50 percent greater risk of dying."[10]

Nearly all of us pray for our mothers and the safety of our children. There is evidence that prayer works even when people don't know that others are praying for them.

A cardiac researcher at St. Luke's Hospital in Kansas City, Dr. William Harris, tested one thousand heart patients who had previously suffered serious cardiac conditions. Without knowing it, half of those patients received daily prayer for two weeks from an intercessory group. The other half received no prayer. Those who were prayed for fared 11 percent better.[11]

More dramatic were the results of a study conducted by a cardiologist at Duke University. Dr. Mitchell Krucoff randomly selected one hundred and fifty heart patients and placed them into five groups, one of which received "off-site intercessory prayer" from other people.

One of the four groups received standard cardiac care, while the others received such varying treatments as stress relaxation, imagery, and touch therapy. Underscoring the power of prayer, those heart patients in the prayer therapy group improved by 50 percent.[12]

Another study at San Francisco General Hospital determined that patients who received prayer were able to leave the hospital sooner than those who didn't.[13]

In the following story, a couple who took The 40 Day Prayer Challenge reported evidence that through its own experiences, prayer really works.

ANSWERED PRAYER—JUST IN TIME

"We were devastated," says Alice. "Fred opened the court orders and read that his former wife was demanding a payment of $300 a week . . . saying she suffered from cancer, had expensive treatments, and couldn't work."

"We didn't have that kind of money," says Fred. "My divorce had been settled a long time before, and Alice and I were starting a new life together. But we were still struggling financially."

"It was about seven o'clock at night. I didn't know what to do," says Alice with an exasperated tone. "So I said, 'Let's get on our knees and pray!' And that's what we did. We'd never prayed before. But we prayed. Hard."

"We had no idea what to expect," adds Fred, but about two and a half hours later the phone rang. *Who's calling this late?* he muttered, lifting the receiver.

It was an anonymous caller identifying himself as someone who had been dating Fred's former wife.

"He started telling me the kind of information to make your hair curl," says Fred, aghast. "He said my former wife had a heavy cocaine habit and would leave her job in the afternoon to go pick up her drugs. He also said she was lying about the cancer and expensive treatments."

"I asked for names and specifics and then had an investigator confirm the charges," continues Fred. "When we presented our case, all demands for money were dropped."

Alice sighs with relief. "It wasn't until we looked back that I said, 'Hey, Fred, do you realize what happened? Our prayers were answered two and a half hours after we got on our knees!'"[14]

Answered Prayers Are Godwinks—
SQuire's Perspective

At various times in this book, Louise and I use the term *godwink*. Because godwinks are related to prayer—particularly as evidence that God answers our prayers in very tangible ways—please let me explain.

Use of the term *godwink* initially appeared in a series of books I authored called *When God Winks* as a substitute for the words *coincidence* or *answered prayer*.

I theorized that if God wished to communicate with humans in a nonaudible way, how would He do it? Through little miracles, I believe. And when these miracles happen, we may find ourselves exclaiming, "Wow, what a coincidence!"

But if you have come to the conclusion that there is no coincidence in coincidences, then what do you call those unbelievable experiences?

Godwinks.

Along the way I also discovered that there is no word in the English language for answered prayer. In other words, if you utter a prayer and God answers it, you have to say a sentence, such as, "God just answered my prayer."

What's the shortcut? For many people, "I just had a godwink" nicely fills the void.

Now, armed with that enlightenment, it might be fun for you to count the number of godwink stories that pop up throughout this book. Many of these stories are delightfully surprising, including the one that follows.

From Olympic Gold to God's Treasure

"I don't know if your son will make it six months if things don't change quickly," the doctor warned Scott's parents.

The illness that had halted Scott's growth from age four to nine—that had him in and out of hospitals, kept him malnourished, and required a steady pattern of dietary supplements—remained a frightening mystery to Scott Hamilton's parents and all the doctors. [15]

"Life was an endless parade of dreary waiting rooms, injection needles, and stethoscopes," remembers Scott of his childhood.

At wits' end about the mysterious illness, famed Boston physician Dr. Harry Schwachman sent nine-year-old Scott back home to Bowling Green, Ohio, with the joyful directive to remove him from all restrictive diets and exercise. Only then did Scott's parents decide to let him participate in Saturday morning skating with his sister and two neighborhood girls.

Wearing a nose tube for food supplements that were still required, Scott strapped on his skates and took to the ice like a bird to the air; he loved it. That's when another mystery, a delightful godwink, began to unfold: he started growing. Doctors concluded that the activity of skating and the cool damp air for his lung condition instigated his miraculous resumption of development.

Although Scott remained the shortest kid in class, he had growth spurts. And soon his strength and agility on ice caused others to take notice.

"For the first time in my life I had self-esteem," says Scott, "because I could do something as well as any other kid."

Another mystery was Scott's muscle development. It was determined that during the five years in which he had no growth, his body had developed no muscles unnecessary to skating.

"I had no excess baggage . . . no bulk from other sports . . . every muscle I had was skating muscle," he says. "And because I was shorter, I was quicker." This was an advantage on issues of technique. "It's a lot easier to correct yourself if you are tiny than if you're tall."

One of Scott's most pleasant mysteries was his audience appeal—the way crowds responded to him so much more than to other skaters. It was resolved that they simply found him cuter and much better than they had expected.[16]

"The only disability in life is a bad attitude," he would later be quoted as saying. And Scott proved that by becoming not just good but the world's most celebrated figure skater. His never-since-equaled winning streak began in 1981 with the first of eight consecutive national and world titles and peaked with the Olympic gold medal at Sarajevo in 1984.[17]

His post-Olympic career has accounted for nearly a dozen television specials and an incredible fifteen years with his own *Stars on Ice* tour.

Then, life threw him a curveball.

In 1997 he was told he had testicular cancer.

"Any cancer diagnosis for anyone is devastating," says Scott. "It's frightening. But I had a great model with the way my mother handled her diagnosis of breast cancer; like her, I tried not to burden anyone with my fears, tried to stay optimistic, surrounding myself with positive people, eliminating negativity."

"I had a stage three tumor," says Scott, adding with determined emphasis, "but I left the doctor's office saying, 'I'm going to beat this thing.'"[18]

He did.

From diagnosis to the next performance was six and a half months.

Now, where was God in all this?

"There's a saying I enjoy: 'God gives us only what we can endure.' I believe life was created to test us to see how much we can handle, and I believe we can endure any hardship or crisis if we put our mind and faith to it."

When Scott Hamilton stepped onto the ice for a CBS Special, *Back on the Ice*, more than ten thousand audience members jumped to their feet and acclaimed their joyful support.

At the end of his performance, amid raucous applause, the crowd was fueled by two words echoing through the arena from Scott's microphone: "I win."

Putting an exclamation point on his performance, he added, "Of course, I wouldn't be all the way back unless . . ." He swiftly completed the statement with an agilely executed signature back flip.

The crowd went wild.[19]

However, Scott Hamilton's upward trajectory still was not devoid of mysteries. Four years later, another one ominously cropped up. But this time, he was fully armed with a prayer warrior at his side; he was deliriously in love with Tracie.

Recently relocated from California, the former Tracie Robinson found herself in an engaging backstage conversation with the Olympic gold medalist at a charity performance of *Stars on Ice* in Memphis. She'd been introduced to Scott by a mutual friend, Tony Thomas of St. Jude Hospital.

"There was a light about him; a sincerity and beauty that I had never seen before in anyone," says Tracie, adding, "I told my cousin Jeana that night, 'Now that's the type of man I see myself marrying.'"

No telephone numbers were exchanged, and when her East Coast job opportunities didn't work out the way she had hoped, Tracie found herself glad to accept an offer from her former employer to move back to the Los Angeles area.

That was just about when Scott, playing golf one day at Hillcrest Country Club with Tony Thomas, said, "What's the story on that girl you introduced me to in Memphis?"

"Funny you should ask; she's moving back here," replied Tony, suggesting that he could get her phone number.

Scott stored the information but did nothing about it.

Then within weeks, another godwink sealed his destiny.

Tracie's only cousin on the West Coast, Jimmy, worked at Sherwood Country Club. She didn't know it, but Scott had known Jimmy for years.

One day Jimmy invited Tracie to a Fourth of July barbeque.

"A lot of fun people will be there . . . Scott Hamilton and . . ."

Tracie heard no other name.

"Scott Hamilton?"

"Yes."

When Jimmy later encountered Scott and told him that his cousin Tracie was coming to the barbeque, he was just as surprised.

"You gotta be kidding! I was just talking with Tony about getting her phone number," exclaimed Scott. "This is amazing."

It was a match made in heaven. Two and a half years later they were married in a beautiful ceremony overlooking Malibu.

Looking back, they've often asked each other what were the odds that Tracie's one West Coast cousin would be working at a country club where Scott Hamilton played golf and that Scott had just inquired about her to Tony Thomas, whom the cousin never knew?

But they've concluded—as each of us does, when we begin to understand godwinks—that with God there's no such thing as odds. Still, God had not fully materialized as an integral part of their new relationship.

"Scott hadn't been going to church and had not dedicated his life to Christ," says Tracie. So she continued to pray about it.

"I prayed so hard," she says, recalling her fervor. "I didn't want to scare him away, but as little things came up I would gently and lovingly try to guide him closer to God. All the while I kept praying, 'Lord, please help me bring him to Christ.'"

At Tracie's nudging, Scott attended church and soon found himself enjoying the experience. He became friends with the pastor and began asking questions about the Bible. From there, Scott's commitment to God grew steadily.

When their son Aidan was born, Scott, the pastor, and other family members gathered around the hospital bed and prayed.

"I will never forget that moment," says Tracie. "It was really beautiful. I felt extremely far from the earth and very close to God. And Scott—himself an adopted child—was being shown so many beautiful things about God, about the miracle of life, and what a blessing it is."

A year later Scott was on the road again when he started feeling ill. It was November 2004, and Tracie had arranged to join him in Cleveland for a cancer benefit.

Before she arrived, Scott decided to schedule tests at the famed Cleveland Clinic.

"When Aidan and I arrived, I could tell something was wrong," says Tracie quietly. "We got into the hotel elevator, and I said, 'Is everything okay?' and he said, 'No, I will tell you.' My mind was racing, and that was the longest elevator ride ever.

"We got to the room, and as Aidan crawled on the floor, Scott said, 'They did some tests this morning. They did a scan, and there's something there. I have a brain tumor, but they don't know much more than that.' I took a deep breath and said, 'Okay, let's pray.' We dropped to our knees and prayed. It was very powerful because God gave us such a peace. And our walk with God became just so extraordinary from that moment on."

While telling us her story, it dawned on Tracie that the moment was even more significant: "That was the first time we ever prayed together, alone, just the two of us, as husband and wife. You're right; prayer is the most intimate act that a husband and wife can experience."

Tracie and Scott began praying that day and never stopped.

"God carried us through that whole time. And as scary as it was, it was also a really extraordinary time. It drew us so much closer. You know, when you think you can't love someone more . . . can't be any closer . . . boy, God really shows you."

Doctors scheduled a biopsy for a week later.

Scott recalls the feelings of uncertainty.

"I remember waking up in the recovery room and thinking, *I know where I am, who I am, and what I'm doing here.* That was one of the most powerful moments I have ever experienced. This medical nightmare was different than my testicular cancer. I had *much* more at stake this time around. But I knew that I had God, Tracie, and Aidan with me this time.

"The doctor then came in and said, 'The tumor is benign. If you had to have a tumor, this is the best option.'"

Their fervent prayers had been answered. Another godwink.

With a tone of relief, Tracie says, "We still had to deal with it—it was still in a very tricky place, but it wasn't cancerous."

"It's been such a blessing," she concludes. "Through the scariest of times, if you pray and are walking with God, He just gives you a calmness and peace that so many in the world don't understand."

Prayer is now a comfortable manifestation in Scott and Tracie's marriage.

"Whenever I'm having a problem situation," says Scott, "I pray for guidance. Then the answer is right there in front of me, every single time."

With a mother's smile, Tracie adds that prayer is also a family experience. "We pray with Aidan all the time, even at two years old. I remember the time that we and some relatives were standing in a circle. Aidan looked up and said, 'Let's pray.'"

Laughing, she then extends her thought: "I want him to know how inspired and comforted you feel when you pray. What a beautiful thing it is."

THE MYSTERIOUS WISDOM OF ANCIENT SCRIPTURES

In this chapter we've discussed impressive evidence to support a belief that God really exists and that prayer really works.

But what about historical verification of the Bible?

For some, the Bible is intimidating and difficult to understand. For others, doubt has emerged: *How do I know for sure that the Ancient Scriptures are accurate? That they weren't just fictional writings of mortal men, long ago?*

For centuries skeptics have attempted to disprove the writings of the Bible.

They've always failed.

How Do We Know the Bible Is True?

The standards we use to test any information we receive are relatively consistent. Believability rises when we read multiple documents, written at different times, from independent sources. The more independent the documentation, the more convincing it is.

Take a news story. If ten different news organizations, totally independent of one another, each sent an investigative reporter to dig into a story and if without talking to each other or comparing notes they all came away with the same basic information, we'd feel as though we could trust it.

The same thing happens as we view history. Events that took place at a time when we could not possibly have personally witnessed them need to be judged by the independent reports that are available for us to evaluate.

The Bible is a collection of sixty-six books, written by forty or more different reporters, over a period of three thousand years.

The first part of the book, the Old Testament, is the basis of the Torah studied in Judaism. The addition of the twenty-seven books of the New Testament, written by a half dozen different reporters over a fifty-year period, creates the Christian Bible.

The number of surviving handwritten manuscripts also validates the events and statements of people in history. It is therefore revealing to compare the number of manuscripts written about various historical personalities whose existence we generally accept.

There are seven known manuscripts about Plato, ten about Caesar, forty-nine about Aristotle, and 24,633 written about the life and times of Christ.

Dr. F. F. Bruce at the University of Manchester asserts, "There is no body of ancient literature in the world which enjoys such a wealth of good textual attestation as the New Testament."[20] Professor Bruce further comments, "If the New Testament were a collection of secular writings, their authenticity would generally be regarded as beyond all doubt."[21]

Another scholar, Sir Frederic Kenyon, has provided this perspective:

> The number of manuscripts of the New Testament . . . is so large that it is practically certain that the true reading of every doubtful passage is preserved in some one or another of these ancient authorities. This can be said of no other ancient book in the world.

He goes on to say,

> Scholars are satisfied that they possess substantially the true text of the principal Greek and Roman writers whose works

have come down to us, of Sophocles, of Thucydides, of Cicero, of Virgil; yet our knowledge depends on a mere handful of manuscripts, whereas the manuscripts of the New Testament are counted by hundreds and even thousands."[22]

Now if that doesn't impress you, consider that most of the stories about Christ were corroborated by various independent writers, reporting at different times: the story of Jesus walking on water was told by three writers—Matthew, Mark, and John—while the story about Jesus feeding more than five thousand people with just five loaves of bread and two fish, with twelve basketsful left over, was reported by Matthew, Mark, Luke, and John.

Yet even though the Bible is the amalgam of so many different writers over thousands of years, it is clearly one book, with unity and consistency throughout. The individual writers had no idea that their contributions would eventually be incorporated into such a document. However, each chapter fits into place and serves a unique purpose as an element of the whole book.

THE POWER OF PROPHECY

A final argument for the truth of the Bible is its 100 percent accuracy in predicting the future. Writer Paul Little contends that these future predictions, called *prophecies*, add scientific evidence to the accuracy of the Bible.

"The prophecies recorded in the Bible came true in such a

detailed way," claims Little, "that they could not have been predicted by chance. Further, archaeologists have evidence that these prophecies were written down (i.e., the Dead Sea Scrolls) many years before they were fulfilled, proving that they were not falsified documents claiming to be prophecies that came true.

"Anyone who diligently studies the Bible will continually find remarkable structural and mathematical patterns woven throughout its fabric, with an intricacy and symmetry incapable of explanation by chance or collusion," says Little.[23]

FINDING POWER
IN THE ANCIENT SCRIPTURES

Throughout the centuries, those who have studied Scripture for the first time in their lives share a common surprise: they are astounded by the wisdom and spiritual fortitude that emerges.

As you take The 40 Day Prayer Challenge, it is a powerful practice to incorporate a daily reading of the Bible with your spouse—either randomly opening the book and reading a chapter or two or methodically reading different books, a chapter at a time or from beginning to end.

To assist you at those times when you don't have a Bible handy, we have selected forty verses that never fail to impart guidance, and placed them for ease of reference at the end of this book.

We recommend that each day, you and your partner digest a bite-sized slice of ageless wisdom about life and living. Ruminate upon it. Discuss it. Live it.

IN THE FINAL ANALYSIS

Famous writer, philosopher, and former atheist C. S. Lewis admitted that he was practicing "willful blindness" when it came to the existence of God, the power of prayer, and the veracity of the Bible.

You probably know some people who turn a blind eye to God. Perhaps they've even derided you for your beliefs.

But you can be secure in knowing that many highly intelligent and gifted people have energetically set out to disprove God. But when they came face-to-face with the overwhelming evidence in favor of God, the power of prayer, and the truth in the timeless writings of the Bible, they have invariably become strong believers.

SECTION

3

FACTORS DURING
YOUR FORTY DAYS

THE DEVIL IS A REAL ENEMY
OF YOUR MARRIAGE

RIGHT FROM WRONG

Comprehending the concept of God is relatively easy. Just look around and count the ways. Gaze at the wondrous form of a baby's foot. Absorb the crescendos of an ocean. Contemplate the petals of a daisy fluttering into the wind. Inhale the sweetness of a rose. Marvel at the intricacies of a robin's nest or the vastness of the Big Dipper on a starry night.

Because you can see, hear, and smell the overwhelming evidence of God everywhere, it is not difficult to enter into a personal relationship with Him, to accept Him as an omnipresent entity in your life. Moreover, even the weakest believers have had a crisis at one time or another when, out of desperation, they've invoked a request for God's intervention.

As exemplified in the last chapter, mounds of evidence is available for anyone willing to see, supporting the facts about the existence, the ministry, and the miracles of Jesus Christ, and the Almighty's existence.

All in all, we have a pretty firm grasp on the goodness of God. We can see the light.

But what about the opposing force of darkness? The force of evil that lurks all around you. Tempts you. Weakens your resistance. *That* force seems less real, more distant, harder to personify.

Even the authors of the Bible have multiple names for what many simply call *the enemy*—Satan, the devil, or the prince of demons.

In the final analysis, we tend to think less about this force of evil as something or someone having a real presence in our lives or . . . as a threat to us.

DEVIL OF DIS—SQUIRE'S PERSPECTIVE

When I was running Children's Television at ABC, an elderly aunt challenged me.

"You need to put some biblical heroes in those Saturday morning cartoons," she stated, pointing a finger to emphasize her seriousness. "Today's kids need to learn values."

I stopped short of attempting to argue with her—to tell her I was running an advertiser-sensitive network daypart; that I had ratings to worry about; that kids wanted to be entertained on

Saturday morning, not feel like they were at another day of school, but . . . I kept my mouth shut, nodded, smiled, and told her I would think about it.

The problem was, I *did* think about it.

Her challenge was almost a dare.

How *could* I introduce basic values into programming targeted to small people who make split-second decisions on what is and isn't boring as rapidly as you can say "click"?

My first reservation was, "*Whose* values should we be teaching them, anyway?"

I thought about the mottos of the Boy and Girl Scouts. Do your best. On your honor. Respect your parents. But they kept returning me to the original top-ten list of values: the Ten Commandments.

Over the next several months, at idle moments during the day, the challenge of my elderly aunt haunted me.

Because I believe all creativity has divine origins, I honestly believe I was awakened in the middle of the night with a divine idea. It was to develop the characters of a program called *The Kingdom Chums*. I saw them as Disneyesque animals representing various values of goodness—love, honesty, and honor—through inborn knowledge they genetically received from ancestors who had witnessed stories at the time of the Bible.

"Every child can comprehend inborn knowledge," I reasoned to my doubtful ABC colleagues. "They accept that dogs are simply born knowing how to bury a bone, and birds just know how to fly south. *The Kingdom Chums* therefore exemplify the values that they have carried instinctively through the ages."

Artwork depicted a small scrappy raccoon named Little David representing the value of courage; his forefather had witnessed the original David-versus-Goliath battle. In another picture, a strong lion named Christopher was the descendant of the lion who witnessed the Christ stories, and so on.

The Kingdom Chums went on the air, amid considerable objections from the network censors in the Standards and Practices department advising me that I had "no right teaching values to children." (Yes, they actually said that.) But I was vindicated when the first prime-time special ratings among kids two to eleven years old turned out to be the highest for any program of the week, on any network.

But my program had one major flaw. *The Kingdom Chums* characters represented only the forces of good.

In order to be true to life for young audiences, I should have invented a character representing the opposing forces of evil. Certainly we all agree that from day to day, we are lured by temptations, seduced by greed, and riddled with anxiety. Additionally, we are infected by negative, unforgiving thoughts. Who causes that?

For future programs, I came up with a character called *Dis of Darkness*.

Dis of Darkness loves everything "dis." He loves distrust, discouragement, and discontent. He cultivates dishonesty, disobedience, and disturbance.

Dis of Darkness comes into our minds and bodies like a viral infection. He disguises himself as something wonderful, something satisfying, something sensuous. And there is only one defense against his evil ways: putting on the full armor of goodness—as exemplified by *The Kingdom Chums*.

Departing after two decades at ABC, I fortunately was able to acquire the rights to *The Kingdom Chums* programs. And having only partially honored the objectives of my elderly aunt, I harbor the notion of developing films and programs that not only will teach kids the values of goodness but also will prepare them, warn them, help them arm themselves against the very real forces of evil. Against the Dis of Darkness.

WALK BY THE LIGHT . . .
SO DARKNESS DOESN'T DESTROY YOU.
IF YOU WALK IN DARKNESS, YOU DON'T KNOW
WHERE YOU'RE GOING . . . BELIEVE IN THE LIGHT.
THEN THE LIGHT WILL BE WITHIN YOU, AND SHIN-
ING THROUGH YOUR LIVES.
YOU'LL BE CHILDREN OF LIGHT.

—JOHN 12:35–36 MSG

REAL LIFE: THE CAPTAIN AND THE DIS

In a true story, famed actor Gavin MacLeod was lured into the clutches of Dis of Darkness. Just as MacLeod's career ship was coming in—starring as the captain of *The Love Boat*, one of television's hottest shows—the enemy lured him and entrapped him.

Patti MacLeod was crushed. Shocked.

Words that had lurked only as the remotest of possibilities

were now right there. Right in her face. Screaming at her. They pierced her heart like a knife.

"I want a divorce."

A ton of bricks dumped on her wouldn't have been as painful. As suffocating. It was like a death in the family.

Gavin's head and heart had been turned. His portrayal of *The Love Boat* captain was the height of his celebrity; he was more recognizable than he'd been in his endearing role as Murray Slaughter on *The Mary Tyler Moore Show*.

Employing the tinsel and treasure of Hollywood, the devil urged Gavin to think only of himself. To party. To have a big house in Beverly Hills. To fly high on the opium of fame and fortune. To put his seven-year marriage to Patti in his rearview mirror.

For Patti it was a tangled mess. Plain and simple. She knew Gavin's decision was a terrible mistake.

The divorce proceeding was like a barefoot trudge through broken glass. Dodging supermarket tabloids splashed with Gavin's pictures, she was in constant mourning, trying to get through one day at a time.

"But I was blessed by having so many wonderful friends," says Patti. They rallied around her . . . gave her support.

"Shirley Boone . . . we'd gotten to know her and her husband Pat . . . called and told me about a group called Born Again Marriage." They assembled regularly, attended by a single partner of a broken marriage.

"When I went to the first meeting at a public school in Westwood, I passed the door thinking I must be in the wrong place," says Patti wryly. "There was a room full of people laughing and having a good time."

But they also spent a good deal of time praying; praying for each other's marriage to get back on course.

Over the next two years Patti became absorbed in learning how to pray and study the Bible. Friends sent her books to read, and she watched television ministries. A prayer partner at a Bible study asked her boldly, "Patti, do you want your husband back?" When Patti nodded, the woman replied assertively, "Well, you can have him back. Let's pray for Gavin."

Patti's confidence rose and her entire demeanor was one of acceptance of a prayer that hadn't yet been answered. She slept only on her side of the bed, leaving Gavin's side and his night-stand untouched. When she sat down to have meals, she set two places, one for her and one for Gavin. And she resumed wearing her wedding ring.

"I prayed for my marriage to be restored, every day, many times a day," says Patti.

Then in September 1984, Patti was shopping with her daughter at a bookstore. She picked up a Bible and thought, *I should buy this for myself.* At the checkout counter she was told that she could emboss a name on the Bible. Without hesitation she said, "Put the name Gavin MacLeod on it."

At home that night, Patti placed the new Bible on Gavin's night table as words from her Bible studies came to mind: "calls things that are not as though they were" (Rom. 4:17).

That was on a Friday.

On Monday, a godwink—Gavin telephoned . . . out of the blue . . . for the first time in three years.

Gavin had just learned that his mother needed a serious operation. Her life was in danger. He promised God that if his mom could be given more time, he would give himself up to Jesus. From the depths of his heart, words—not his own—directed him: *Call Patti.*

Somehow all the fame and fortune had been empty promises. All the parties were vacuous. All the glitter was gone. Only the image of Patti . . . the security of a loving wife . . . a home with hearth and heart . . . seemed suddenly real.

He called her, told her about his mom, and then blurted, "When can I see you?"

Patti paused, sensing the wonder of the godwink that was unfolding before her—God's answer to her prayers.

Her mind went to her schedule. She was traveling for the next few days.

"How about in a week?"

It felt odd when, a week later, Gavin approached the door of his former home with Patti. He was apprehensive as he raised his hand to rap on the door. *Would she still want to see him?*

There was no answer.

Maybe she had second thoughts.

He knocked again.

She must hate me. I don't blame her!

And again, almost ready to give up.

The door opened.

There she was, as sweet and radiant as always, carrying herself with an air of familiar self-confidence and a dash of wry humor.

She smiled.

"I'm sorry your dinner's cold," she said. "It's been waiting three years."

⚜

A FEW MONTHS later there was a wedding. Their second marriage—
to each other. God's plan unfolded so unimaginably, it could only
have been authored by Him. Rather than the small, private wedding they'd talked about, they were persuaded to hold their ceremony in public—at a convention in Omaha.

Auspiciously, it was the annual meeting of Born Again Marriages. There, with Pat and Shirley Boone as their best man and
matron of honor, Gavin and Patti witnessed to hundreds of others the power of faith and prayer to heal a marriage that had gone
off course.

A short time after that, Gavin and Patti appeared on a TBN
telecast. During their visit to the studios, network founder Paul
Crouch was struck with a divine notion—a godwink: "Why don't
you two host a marriage show for us?"

And that's what they did. For the next decade and a half,
Gavin and Patti MacLeod's weekly show brought hope to millions
of couples. It was, appropriately, called *Back on Course*.

GET RID OF THE DIS IN YOUR LIFE—LOUISE'S PERSPECTIVE

You are in a battle for your marriage!

There is a mastermind working 24/7 to destroy it.

The Bible says he's like a roaring lion, prowling around seeing whom he can devour (1 Peter 5:8).

As my husband described him, he's the Dis of Darkness who

will pull out all stops to convince you to dishonor, disbelieve, and distance yourself from your partner. He's a deceiver and a liar.

If he can drag you into divorce court, he's done his job.

Dis of Darkness uses many different traps to trip you up. One of his wily ways is to mess with your mind. He wants you to feel discouraged about your marriage. Disillusioned. Disappointed. Sometimes he even plants a notion in your mind that you deserve something better. Soon he has you fantasizing about someone other than your spouse.

The devil tells you it's perfectly fine to fantasize about another person because it's not real. He fills your brain with rationalizations. He's even led the mental health community to dispense an unproven notion that it's perfectly healthy to fantasize about someone other than your partner.

Not true!

THE BIG LIE—SQUIRE'S PERSPECTIVE

I recall the first time I heard a marriage counselor suggest that fantasizing about someone other than your spouse, and the self-pleasuring that often follows, was wrong.

Wrong? *How could this be?* I wondered.

I'd heard just the opposite on television talk shows and read magazine articles promoting the alleged benefits of fantasy and erotic videos. There was a chorus of acceptability by psychologists and marital advisors that viewing pornographic videos with your partner would "spice up your love life" and that masturbation while fantasizing about someone outside of your marriage was "perfectly natural and healthy."

And here this one counselor was saying it was wrong. Why? He used logic.

First, many of us have come to know that thoughts are *things*. Our entire existence follows the pattern of our thoughts.

Secondly, most of us would agree that adultery is severely destructive to a marriage. If that's the case, why then would *mental* adultery be good for you?

"Think about it," he said. "If God has given you and your spouse the gift of lovemaking, an extraordinary joy to be shared privately and exclusively with each other, why would cheating on your partner in a movie in your mind be anything but detrimental?"

The penny dropped for me.

The popular notion that the mental health industry has bought into is simply a big lie. And a big victory for Dis of Darkness.

PORN ADDICTION

Pornography is the "most concerning thing to psychological health . . . existing today," testified Dr. Mary Anne Layden before the Senate Commerce Committee's Science, Technology and Space Subcommittee. The codirector of the Sexual Trauma and Psychopathology Program for the University of Pennsylvania's Center for Cognitive Therapy went on to say, "The Internet is a perfect drug delivery system because you are anonymous, aroused, and have role models for these behaviors."

There is a massive and growing body of scientific evidence that shows that when we look at illicit material, a chemical is actually released in our brains that is highly addictive.

Citing the addictive nature of porn, Dr. Layden said, "To have a drug pumped into your house 24/7, free, and children know how to use it better than grown-ups know how to use it, it's a perfect delivery system . . ."

Dr. Layden contends that pornography addicts have a more difficult time recovering from their addiction than cocaine addicts since coke users can get the drug out of their systems while pornographic images stay in the brain forever.[1]

In marriage, the more you allow your mind to focus on those images, the more enslaved you become and the more you distance yourself from your partner. The enemy works that way. Just a little thought about someone other than your partner pops into your head, and that thought becomes like a cancer; it keeps spreading until it takes over your entire being and directs your actions.

"Research also indicates . . . that 40 percent of sex addicts will lose their spouses," reported Dr. Layden, while "58 percent will suffer severe financial losses, and 27 to 40 percent will lose their job."

She also divulged a shocking statistic to the U.S. senators: "Research indicates that 70 percent of the hits on Internet sex sites occur between 9 a.m. and 5 p.m. on business computers."[2]

Who says porn is not addictive?

How Do You Deal with Temptation?

The Bible advises us to "put on the whole armor of God, that you may be able to stand against the wiles of the devil" (Eph. 6:11 NKJV) and to "resist the devil, and he will flee from you" (James 4:7).

FORGIVENESS POWER

Forgiveness is a gift you give yourself. It can be unwrapped only after you fully forgive someone who has wronged you, or when you ask someone for his forgiveness.

Whether or not that person accepts or grants forgiveness is not what's important. What counts is your giving it or asking for it.

WHY IS FORGIVING SO HARD TO DO?

You see, forgiveness is not about the other person; it is all about you and your relationship with God.

Furthermore, forgiveness is the key to unlocking blessings for yourself. According to the timeless wisdom of the Bible, giving or asking forgiveness will release God's blessings in a torrent of power that you would never have imagined.

One of the biblical biographers, Mark, quotes Jesus as saying, "But when you are praying, first forgive anyone you are holding a grudge against, so that your Father in heaven will forgive your sins, too."[1]

THE FREQUENCY OF FORGIVENESS

How often should we forgive or ask to be forgiven? Every day.

Think back to one of the first prayers you ever memorized. "Give us this day our daily bread. And forgive us our debts, as we forgive our debtors."[2] Those were the instructions, directly from the Master through the Lord's Prayer.

We once heard famed pastor Charles Stanley note in one of his broadcasts that the words *give us . . . our* daily *bread* and *forgive us . . .* means we need to ask God not only for food on a daily basis but also to ask for and give forgiveness on a daily basis as well. It's that important.

WHO PUSHES YOUR BUTTONS?

Let's take this out of the theoretical and put it into the practical.

Do you have someone in your life who riles you because of his manner of speaking to you or others? Someone who *pushes your buttons*? Someone you've been resenting, for one reason or another?

Never mind whether or not you were in the right. The question is . . . are you harboring old grudges?

Have you found yourself keeping a secret list of your grievances? During a squabble, have you heard yourself say "you never" or "you always" do this or that?

Those are all pretty good signals that you've been carrying around resentments like gum on the bottom of your shoe; you don't quite know how to shake them off. And if you're like the rest of us, you may have hidden your lack of forgiveness so deep that you don't even realize you've been carrying it for years, like baggage that's turned into a permanent backpack.

In the following story, we can empathize with John's difficulty in forgiving someone who had wounded him. But no one could have predicted the clear sign of assurance from above—the godwink—when he finally did.

Forgiveness—A Hard Pill to Swallow

John Griffin was a twenty-five-year-old entrepreneur when the bottom fell out of his life. His small swimming pool construction firm was flying high one moment, and he was looking at bankruptcy the next.

The problems began when he hired someone he thought he could trust—a woman he'd known all his life—to run the office and pay the bills while he went into the field to acquire new business and oversee pool construction. But in the course of six weeks, he discovered that the *trusted* person had drained his cash reserves of $120,000, writing a series of $20,000 checks to herself.

Within weeks John lost his business, his cars, and his home.

"I didn't have two nickels to rub together," says John.

But one thing he did have was hate.

"I hated the person who had robbed my life," he says with emphasis, "and I hated myself for the horrible mistakes I had made."

John's work ethic remained exemplary, however, and by bearing down, taking multiple sales jobs that required no withholding taxes, and by filing tax extensions for the next three years, he was able to pay back his debts and get back on track.

"For three years I didn't speak to the person who embezzled all that money from me," says John with tightened lips. "But at my dad's funeral, she came up to me in tears and asked for my forgiveness."

"Here was the person who had caused me to lose everything, asking me to forgive her. I looked her right in the eyes . . . and said . . . 'I forgive you.'"

But walking away, John felt a spirit quicken within him. A voice representing deep resentment said, *You haven't forgiven her.*

Oh, yes, I have, John began to argue.

No, you haven't, the voice argued back.

Several months passed without John encountering the offending person again.

Then, out of the blue, he received a telephone call.

It was the embezzler, adding insult to injury: "I don't know who to call," she said. "I need six hundred dollars to pay the rent or I'm going to be evicted."

Before slamming the phone down in a burst of fury, John uttered two words unacceptable for polite company.

See? I told you, you didn't forgive her.

It was the return of the inner voice.

Yes, I have, claimed John, *but I'm sure not giving her any money!*

An hour later John began to soften.

An hour after that, he stood at the Western Union counter to wire money.

John had remembered something his dad once shared with him. "He would stuff coat and pants pockets with small amounts of money . . . five or ten dollars here . . . twenty dollars there. He called it his 'little stash of loot' for those times when he needed it."

John had followed in his father's footsteps. And after that inner voice had worn him down, he went fishing through pockets in his closet. The amount he found was six hundred and twenty dollars. Now, at the Western Union counter, the clerk told him the cost of wiring the money would be twenty dollars. All told, it was the exact amount needed to satisfy the woman's request.

He then placed a call on his cell phone to the recipient.

"Look for a Western Union wire for six hundred dollars," he said, hanging up with the satisfaction he'd done the right thing, even though he remained doubtful that it was a desirable thing to do.

His telephone rang. He could tell by the caller ID that it was his tax accountant. His heart sank. This was the call he had been dreading. The shoe was about to drop on how much he owed in back taxes.

"David, just say the number and hang up so I can die by myself," he sighed into the phone.

On the other end of the line, David laughed.

"You're not going to believe this . . . but you're owed a refund," said the accountant.

"What?"

"I went back and recalculated your returns for the past three years," said David with a note of self-satisfaction, "and by applying your losses to subsequent years, you're due a refund."

"Really? How much?"

"About $6,200."

If John ever needed a confirming godwink that he had done the right thing, this was it. He was being rewarded with ten times the amount of money he had just spent to affirm his forgiveness of someone who had wronged him.

RELEASING RESENTMENT BALLOONS

What can you do about resentments you've been carrying around—those scarred-over grudges? Ask God to reveal them to you. And once they're identified, you can release them back to God in prayer.

> PETER: HOW OFTEN SHALL I
> FORGIVE HIM? SEVEN TIMES?
>
> JESUS: NOT SEVEN TIMES, BUT UP
> TO SEVENTY TIMES SEVEN.[3]

Picture the name of each person related to a resentment written on a balloon, tethered to a string in your hand. One by one, tell God you are letting go of the string, and imagine each resentment balloon soaring up to Him . . . no longer in your grasp.

Avoid reaching out, grabbing that string, and reeling your resentments right back into your possession. If that happens, just start again. Again ask God for forgiveness, and again let go of the string holding the resentment, letting it rise heavenward.

If you search your emotions for a new sense of comfort, and find that you don't feel anything, don't be surprised. You see, forgiveness is not about feelings. It's about obedience. And the very act of your obedience—releasing the resentment by asking for or giving forgiveness—will unleash God's blessings to you.

When you forgive your spouse or others who have wounded you, God will draw you into a more intimate fellowship with Him.

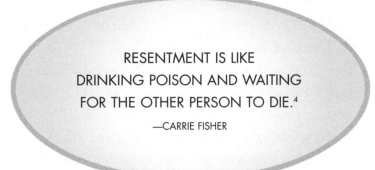

RESENTMENT IS LIKE
DRINKING POISON AND WAITING
FOR THE OTHER PERSON TO DIE.[4]
—CARRIE FISHER

In retrospect, many of us will conclude that our resentments were blown up in our minds. Like letting go of those balloons, in time they diminish in size and are totally out of sight.

Sometimes, of course, people will suffer huge assaults on their psyche . . . so large that forgiveness seems impossible. Imagine if you found out that your wife was suspected of having an affair with the minister.

FORGIVE THE PASTOR

"I guess I'm going to have to kill the pastor," said her husband softly.

Paula looked at Jeff to study his degree of outrage.

Is he joking . . . actually joking? Or is he serious?

How do you spill your guts to your husband of eight years that you've been having an affair of the heart and mind with the pastor? And even though you never cheated physically, you may have to move out of town anyway?

It started so innocently.

Paula had been attending the new church alone because her husband, Jeff, was not a Christian.

The pastor was a terrific speaker and a wonderful singer with an engaging knack for occasionally interrupting his sermon, sitting at the piano, and singing part of his message.

Paula's growth curve as a novice Christian was exhilarating! She quickly became actively involved in the church, loved the Bible studies, and told everyone what a wonderful experience it was.

Perhaps the first crossing of a line—or "going through a red light" as she would say later in her book—was when her lunches to chat with the pastor became more frequent.[5]

"I was a happily married woman, a doting mother, and a

strong Christian," says Paula. "That's why nothing could have prepared me for what happened next."

One of her favorite services of the week was on Sunday nights. While Jeff stayed home with her son, she'd attend the uplifting service of music and worship, usually lasting until ten or eleven o'clock.

Charged with excitement, a smaller group would break off afterward with the pastor and his wife and go to Denny's restaurant.

Paula would call Jeff from the parking lot. Did he mind if she went with the others?

"His voice said okay, but his tone whispered no," says Paula. "It was one of the many red lights I eventually drove right through."

She really liked the pastor. And it was mutual. The conversations were charming and witty. "We could laugh and talk for hours," she says.

Eventually the pastor began to telephone her each day while his wife was taking an afternoon nap with the children. More red lights.

Did she tell Jeff about these afternoon calls? No. They were secret. Redder red lights.

The enemy whispered in her mind that this was all innocent. After all, she and the pastor had never even touched. Hadn't even shaken hands. But the pastor's admiration and attention was flattering; it made her feel good about herself. She enjoyed the role of *favorite* in his flock of sheep.

What started to bring Paula to her senses?

It was the dream. In her dream she saw the pastor approaching her and heard a voice she identified as God's: "You are spending too much time together."

That shook her.

Up to that point Paula had confided in no one. She telephoned an old friend in another city. Her friend's counsel was swift and direct: "Leave that church immediately . . . run."

Instead, Paula just ran the red light again.

What's the problem here? Just a little harmless flirting, she told herself.

But the red light that finally brought Paula to a screeching halt was the day the pastor confided that his interest in her "was more than just a friend."

"I had played with fire; now I was getting burned," says Paula. "I had no intention of having a sexual fling with this man. I was just enjoying a little harmless flattery . . . but now I was in deep trouble."

Not long after that, the too-close relationship between Paula and the pastor surfaced with the board of elders. She was called before them and abruptly asked to leave the church. Immediately and permanently.

The elders also met with the pastor in an unsuccessful attempt to encourage restoration, but eventually, he and his family moved to another community.

For Paula, the longest bridge was yet to be crossed. She had to tell Jeff—to ask for her husband's forgiveness.

"Jeff was understandably hurt and angry," she says, recalling how she searched his face for meaning to his response:

"I guess I'll have to kill the pastor."

Did he mean that?

"Yes, he meant it—for a moment," she says.

But Jeff was relieved that nothing physical had happened between his wife and the pastor. And he believed her.

"In a small town where nobody believed me, it was a great gift that my husband believed me," says Paula.

And then, he forgave her.

Paula and Jeff began repairing their relationship.

"As I began focusing on my own home, my husband became my best friend," she says.

Meanwhile, it was traumatizing for Paula to begin attending another church. As a show of support, Jeff began to accompany her on Sunday mornings.

As he became more and more invested in his own faith, he came to understand the extraordinary power of prayer and became a Christian. Together they began discovering an exhilarating bonding through the almost indescribable intimacy of prayer.

With the pain of Paula's emotional affair in the distance, Paula and Jeff had experienced the extraordinary power of forgiveness between the two of them, yet Jeff had not arrived at the point where he was willing to forgive the pastor.

Paula encountered a health crisis. As a couple, God's help was sought.

When she recovered and they took stock of the incredible blessing God had bestowed upon them, Jeff looked into Paula's eyes and said, "Now I'm going to have to choose to forgive him, aren't I?"

She nodded.

"He felt relief after that choice," says Paula.

Today, Paula and Jeff enjoy the unequaled joy of joint prayer.

"The intimacy of couples praying is like none other," she says. "For instance, no one on earth feels exactly the same way I feel about our children—except my husband. My husband is, therefore, my covering. Our joint prayers create not only a greater closeness, but they build a fortress of protection around us."

I CAN FORGIVE, BUT I CANNOT FORGET, IS ONLY ANOTHER WAY OF SAYING, I WILL NOT FORGIVE. FORGIVENESS OUGHT TO BE LIKE A CANCELLED NOTE—TORN IN TWO . . .[6]

—HENRY WARD BEECHER

8

PRAYER AND MONEY

It is estimated that 50 percent of all divorces are caused by financial problems. Maybe that's why nearly half the parables in the Bible relate to money, possessions, or debt.

When you face uncertainty about being able to pay your bills and you're uncertain that your family is safe and secure, you have stress. And financial stress causes cracks in the very foundations of your marriage.

It's easy to see how the forces of darkness would use financial problems to erode your marriage, causing tension and fostering arguments. The last thing the devil wants is a happy marriage, free of financial woes.

Moreover, the society we live in lures us into buying more

and more *things*. Credit card companies constantly devise new ways to *buy now, pay later.*

Only when you are staring at the mounting debt do you come to the realization that some credit cards may have been socking you for as much as 28 percent interest on delinquent accounts.

Just remember this: When your back is to the wall, you're not where God wants you. You're in enemy territory. God wants to get you out.

Is It Okay to Pray for Money?

Yes!

You've heard the saying "money is the root of all evil." But the Bible tells us that it's the *love* of money where the root begins (1 Timothy 6:10). God's plan is to give you financial freedom. Therefore, praying for financial security and guidance is something God wants for you.

In the following story, Tiffany and Matt, who have taken The 40 Day Prayer Challenge, discovered that through the power of prayer, they were able to break the financial concerns that had clutched them.

God's Turnaround

"In the beginning, we were under attack every day," says Tiffany. "We started our forty days of prayer, and one thing after another started weighing down on us."

Tiffany and Matt had been married nearly two years. During that time, plenty of things had happened that they prayed about—Tiffany was trying to find her own career path, and Matt stepped out in faith to start his own painting company. Both were focused on trying to have a baby and start a family, but daily prayer *together* had never been suggested to them.

"I knew if Satan was attacking us just as we were starting our prayer challenge, we must be doing something right for the Lord," concludes Tiffany.

"The very day we began, I got a summons to appear at a court arbitration in Philadelphia," says Matt, adding that it was a four-hour drive to get there.

"We couldn't believe it," says Tiffany. "Matt had been in an accident in Philadelphia seven years earlier—a cab driver ran a red light and broadsided Matt's car. The cabbie was clearly at fault, and now he was trying to sue Matt," she continues with astonishment.

"Fortunately I wasn't hurt, but the force of the collision sent my car into a pizza shop," remembers Matt.

The accident, which had happened in 2000, was clearly an important item in their daily prayer. The young couple was worried about the outcome. Could Matt find witnesses to support him seven years later? Would the court find in his favor, or would he be required to come up with a huge monetary settlement with the cab driver?

Starting with five minutes a day and extending their prayer time accordingly, Tiffany and Matt talked to God almost every day about the stress they felt about the impending court case as well as other issues, including their mounting concern that Tiffany wasn't getting pregnant.

Matt had a lawyer assigned to him by his insurance company. The attorney repeatedly pressed Matt to search his memory for supportive witnesses and evidence.

"I called the owner of the pizza shop," says Matt. "I knew him, because I used to go in there all the time. I was sure he'd support me. But I was disappointed to learn that he'd just left for Greece for several months. I was worried. The arbitration was getting closer and I had no witnesses."

The huge financial uncertainty over the court case loomed over them like a dark cloud. The question echoing in their minds was, *What if we lose and have to come up with some ridiculous amount of money?*

On the day of Matt's court appearance, they both took off from work and drove to Philadelphia.

A panel of three stern-faced lawyers sat at a table in the arbitration room.

The cabbie and his lawyer were first to present their case against Matt. The cabbie attempted to foster sympathy. He told the panel that his wife had died. That he had mounting doctors' bills resulting from the accident. He said that he was driving three or four car-lengths behind another car when Matt drove through the intersection and plowed into him. He showed photos of his damaged cab.

Matt's lawyer cross-examined the cabbie, noting that the photos showed his car was damaged in the front end, not the side.

Still, Matt was worried. He had no witnesses to support his story, which was that the cabbie was lying, that *he* was the one who was to blame.

One of the lawyers then signaled that it was Matt's turn to

present his side of the case. In a voice attempting to hide the anxiety that churned within, Matt began his testimony.

Suddenly Matt was interrupted by a remarkable godwink— one of those moments when you just know God has intervened in His own special way, just to let you know that it's Him.

One of the lawyers on the panel cut in.

"Wait a minute. When did this accident happen? In 2000? Were you in a car that crashed into a pizza shop?" asked the lawyer.

Matt nodded.

"I was there! I saw that accident that day!" exclaimed the lawyer.

Shortly thereafter the panel of lawyers advised that they would meet privately and that the participants would be notified once a judgment had been made.

Before Tiffany and Matt were halfway back to their home near Norfolk, Virginia, Matt received a phone call from his attorney.

The court had found in his favor.

Tiffany wrote in her journal, "You gave Matt a peace. We just wanted the truth to be heard and it was. We won. Praise God!"

Once again, Tiffany and Matt discovered the power of jointly bringing their worries to the Lord through prayer. The astonishing godwink was evidence that God heard them and was the supreme judge in this case.

But that was not all.

A few days after their forty days of prayer ended, Tiffany excitedly exclaimed, "Oh, my gosh!"

Matt ran from the other room to see what was the matter.

She had just taken the digital test and it registered "pregnant."

"We are going to have a baby!" they shouted in unison, embracing each other for a long time. They cried. Then they thanked the Lord.

How Do I Get Out of Debt?

Financial problems usually start from job loss, poor health, or simply poor money management and living beyond your means.

In your daily prayer, ask God to clarify the things you can get along without, in order to focus on the things you need. Ask Him to help you discipline yourself with a budget and open the way for professional help.

WITH GOD'S POWER WORKING IN US, GOD CAN DO MUCH, MUCH MORE THAN ANYTHING WE CAN ASK OR IMAGINE.

—EPHESIANS 3:20 NCV

Should We Pray for New Jobs or Career Opportunities?

Absolutely.

Asking for assistance from above leading you to a new job opportunity, income source, or clarification on what career moves you should be making are all within the scope of what you and your partner should be praying about.

Get specific. Communicate with God about specific financial needs you have, and expect to receive an answer.

POSSIBILITIES TO PROBABILITIES
IS PURE MUSIC

Their careers had been inching along like Los Angeles traffic—moments when you shoot ahead, then inexplicably everything slows down and you find yourself waiting for something totally out of your control to get you moving again.

Mari Falcone had inhaled the sweet smell of success. Emerging from the suburbs of Chicago, she had trained as a concert pianist then found that her no-nonsense personality was perfectly suited to work as a musical director for major artists. With a love for R&B and gospel music, her conducting and composing subsequently led her to work with performers such as Donna Summer, Nell Carter, Debby Boone, Amy Grant, and Deniece Williams.

"As an artist and as a woman there are two very different sides of my personality," admits Mari. "One side is very lyrical and sensitive, and the other" . . . she pauses for emphasis and a mischievous smile, "just wants to kick butt."

Mari's husband, Bill Cantos, is also a remarkable musician. With a master's in music from Boston's New England Conservatory, he surfaced as an accomplished composer, vocalist, and keyboard artist, touring with Phil Collins, Herb Alpert, and Sergio Mendes.

Together Mari and Bill have become a musical force leading worship in churches and performing in secular clubs and concert halls, putting their albums in demand.

Still, Mari's and Bill's careers were stuck in L.A. traffic.

Fast lane, slow lane. Stop. Go.

Many of their prayers remained unfulfilled.

Then they began The 40 Day Prayer Challenge.

"With our prayer list we could think big," says Mari, her long red hair bouncing as she accentuates *big*.

"Who knew we were entering a season when God would throw open windows and doors of opportunity?" marvels Bill.

During the first week of The 40 Day Prayer Challenge, Mari and Bill explicitly prayed that their careers would crystallize in very specific ways . . . that their stalled projects would have new life and new direction.

Then they started meeting people whose paths they previously had never crossed, people who championed their music and were doing precisely the kind of work in the entertainment industry they wanted.

Within weeks of composing their prayer list, Mari and Bill were excitedly discussing new projects that would have seemed unthinkable just a few months earlier.

"God has given us such favor," claims Bill.

"This is such a huge leap," gasps Mari. "We don't feel at all ill prepared, but it's awesome how God is taking us out of one place and putting us into another. He has given us such *unbelievable* favor!"

Beep. Beep. Mari and Bill just moved into the express lane.

Does Money Bring Happiness?

If you were to interview a few dozen lottery winners, you might be surprised to learn that money never brought them the happiness they expected.

All too often, what they thought was the American dream turned into a nightmare. Some lottery winners even become bankrupt, and that's not happiness.

Let's Talk About Tithing

You may know what tithing *is*, but the question is: what's in it for you?

Before really understanding the true principles of tithing, most of us have simply shrugged and said we'd *love* to give away money to a good cause . . . if we were Bill Gates or Warren Buffet . . . but, frankly, we need every cent we have.

To begin with, the concept of tithing isn't just about money. And it's not about other people. It's about *you*, and what happens to you when you give to others.

It may be money that you give or possessions such as contributions to the church bazaar. But tithing could also be the giving of your time in volunteer service. Or it might be giving away anything you have that others might find valuable, such as a list of contacts to help someone get started in a new job.

Tithing is giving back. It's an act of love and obedience that God expects of you. And when you do give back, as exemplified in the following story with John and Angela, He acknowledges it and rewards you.

TITHE (NOUN)

- ONE-TENTH OF ANNUAL PRODUCE OR EARNINGS, FORMERLY TAKEN AS A TAX FOR THE SUPPORT OF THE CHURCH AND CLERGY.
- IN CERTAIN RELIGIOUS DENOMINATIONS, A TENTH OF AN INDIVIDUAL'S INCOME PLEDGED TO THE CHURCH.[1]

—AMERICAN HERITAGE DICTIONARY

WE DON'T OWN OUR STUFF—IT OWNS US

It was an indelible lesson for five-year-old John, perched upon his daddy's lap, analyzing his father's monthly ritual of writing checks to pay the bills.

"Johnny, look here," said his father, a veteran Disney character actor. "The first 10 percent goes to the Lord. That's called tithing."

"I can still remember my dad saying that," says John Griffin, an enthusiastic thirty-six-year-old businessman.

John and his wife, Angela, are telling us about the time they lived in a big house, drove big cars, and were racking up mountains of debt, while John, through his father's example, was secretly tithing.

"We had separate checking accounts," admits John. "Angela never knew how much I tithed, but when she found out, we had some knock-down, drag-out fights."

Angela, an attractive, blonde businesswoman with a wisp of Georgia accent, explains: "I grew up without a lot of money. I saw him writing out a check to the church that could have been a week's salary for somebody, and that was really hard for me."

As John and Angela's intoxication with the high life continued, surfing on an ever-larger wave of debt, Angela grew more worried. To contribute to the family income, she studied for her real-estate license, became a broker, and then started her own agency. She, more than John, was uneasy with their debt and sensed the need to conserve what income they had.

She looked around herself one day, and arrived at a drastic conclusion.

"I realized we were married to our stuff. All our stress and worries were in reference to getting enough money to collect more stuff or pay for the stuff we had. So, when John came home, I said, 'Let's get rid of the stuff.'"

The idea was a bit shocking to John.

"When Angela said, 'We don't own our stuff. It owns us. Let's get rid of everything.' God may have been working on her, but I was thinking, *I don't want to get rid of my Hummer. I don't want to move out of my house. I like watching TV downstairs in my theater*. But then, after a few weeks, I said, 'All right, we'll do it.'"

The following weekend John left for a men's retreat.

"It was the wildest thing," he says. "When I got home, Angela said, 'Hey, I've got good news. I listed the house . . . didn't even get to put a sign in front . . . and sold it to the first person who looked at it.'"

After a series of garage sales reduced their furnishings, Angela and John moved out of their six-thousand-square-foot home into a sixteen-hundred-square-foot condo, one-quarter the size.

Steadily their finances began to even out, and they pulled themselves from the clutches of debt. And while Angela was now comforted that their finances were managed in the open with a joint checking account, the concept of giving away the firstfruits of their income, a 10 percent slice to help others, remained difficult for her. She cautiously accepted John's reasoning that the Lord will reward you tenfold when you tithe, but that idea quickly flipped back into being wholly irrational when she calculated the shortfall remaining in the monthly budget.

"I'm still a work in progress," she admits.

Then a pivotal godwink occurred.

The pastor's sermon was a bit dry that Sunday morning in church. Angela's mind wandered to thoughts about her new real estate business. She ruminated about the marketing course she'd taken the week before, which instructed business owners to offer something to their customers that no one else was providing— "your unique proposition."

"As I was sitting in the pew, the light bulb went off," exclaims Angela. "Give away 10 percent of every commission!"

"When my wife told me we're going to tithe 10 percent off the top of every sale, I immediately got on that wagon," says John. "I knew it must have come from God, because my wife would have never said that."

Angela began the new business policy the next day, pledging to all new clients that 10 percent of the sales commission would be given to the church or charity of their choice.

"I found that people were very encouraged to be doing business with someone who had the integrity to give away some of the money, to pay it forward," says Angela.

Yet she continued to struggle with feelings of weakness.

"I decided the money would come off the top, before I had a choice. I knew if the money ever made it to my banking account, I would not want to part with it."

Almost overnight her tithing was rewarded.

"My business began to grow, rapidly," she says.

John makes another observation.

"In business, your best lead is a referral. Because Angela had made sure that every check was written directly to the pastor or the head of the charity, she kept getting great referrals from those people—prospects who were new in the area, or people who were selling their houses."

Soon word got out, and brokers from around the country were calling Angela, asking for advice on how they, too, could adopt the radical business idea of giving away 10 percent off the top of their commissions.

How did tithing repay them tenfold as the Bible promises?

More than a half dozen houses that John and Angela had purchased as business investments to fix up for resale suddenly started selling.

"It showed us that you can't out-give God," says John. "When Angela realized we were honoring our stuff and not God, and then committed to tithing, our lives changed dramatically."

In the final analysis, God gave Angela and John more blessings than they had in the first place. The house they gave up was six-thousand square feet. They now live in a thirteen-thousand-square-foot house.

But this is the big difference: their stuff no longer owns them.

WHOEVER SOWS SPARINGLY WILL ALSO REAP SPARINGLY, AND WHOEVER SOWS GENEROUSLY WILL ALSO REAP GENEROUSLY. EACH MAN SHOULD GIVE WHAT HE HAS DECIDED IN HIS HEART TO GIVE, NOT RELUCTANTLY OR UNDER COMPULSION, FOR GOD LOVES A CHEERFUL GIVER.

—2 CORINTHIANS 9:6–7

WHAT HAPPENS WHEN YOU TITHE?

God's blessings are released to you.

Before raising a doubtful eyebrow, prepare yourself for some very persuasive facts.

Let's start with the Ancient Scriptures. The only place in the Bible where God has challenged you to test Him is as follows:

"Bring the whole tithe into the storehouse, that there may be food in my house. Test me in this," says the LORD Almighty, "and see if I will not throw open the floodgates of heaven and pour out so much blessing that you will not have room enough for it."—Malachi 3:10

When God says "test me," we'd better know that He means business.

Go ahead, give at least 10 percent of your finances, your time, and/or your talents, and see what God does in your life. The more you give to God, the more He will give to you. You simply cannot out-give God. Try it!

THE WORLD'S MOST SUCCESSFUL AUTHOR

Rick Warren is the author of the all-time best-selling hardcover book *The Purpose Driven Life*. About forty million copies have been sold to date.

But Rick's main job is the pastor of a church in Southern California. As his extracurricular activities as a writer began producing income rivaling his ministerial salary, he and his wife, Kay, began increasing their tithe.

"When we got married thirty years ago, we began tithing 10 percent. Each year we would raise our tithe 1 percent to stretch our faith: 11 percent the first year, 12 percent the second year, 13 percent the third year," explains Rick.

He says that each time he gave, he found that it would break the grip of materialism on his life. He and Kay became reverse tithers.

"Every time I give, my heart grows bigger. And so now, we give away 90 percent, and we live on 10 percent."[2]

Once asked by TV interviewer Larry King, "Is it a sin to be rich?" Rick Warren replied with a smile, "No, it's a sin to die rich."

GENEROSITY REWARDS

People who are generous with their money are much more joyful, says Susan McCarthy. The author of *The Value of Money* contends that those who give generously see their kindness reciprocated with other good fortune in their lives.

On a personal level she noticed this when she decided to help out a school by giving it some shares of stock in an account that she'd nearly overlooked. Shortly after she gave away the stock, the remaining stock in her portfolio rose to fill the vacancy in the account.

"I notice that whenever I use funds from that stock to help those in need, that my little pool of stock is always replenished. It's like a little fountain that's always there. Of course, there are no guarantees when it comes to stocks but nonetheless, that's the way it has worked out," she says.

Oftentimes, using our possessions generously will return benefits in other ways.

Susan cites a friend who purchased a motor home then faced the knotty problem of where to park it. It was too big to leave it in her driveway. And the neighbors, she feared, would not find the giant vehicle an attractive addition to the street.

The friend then had a wonderful idea borne of a generous heart. She made an arrangement with a local children's hospital to allow her to park the RV in their parking lot, in return for allowing the vehicle to be used at the hospital's discretion for families of hospitalized children.

Her friend's outcome is the joy of knowing she's helping others who are hurting, while being able to use her motor home anytime she wants.

"Having money is not a bad thing," says Susan. "It depends on what we do with it. Money is only a tool with no intrinsic power. We *give* it the power."

THERE IS A PLACE WHERE GIVING IS PAINLESS AND RECEIVING IS SELFLESS. FIND THAT PLACE IN YOUR OWN LIFE, AND MOVE TOWARDS IT. AS YOU DO . . . YOUR SCARCITY THINKING WILL DISSOLVE, AND A MINDSET OF ABUNDANCE WILL FLOW THROUGH YOUR REALITY.[3]

—STEVE PAVLINA

SIX STEPS TO A HAPPY MARRIAGE

This book got started with the seminar we've done for the last several years as husband and wife, Everything I Know About Wrecking Relationships, I Learned in My Last Marriage.

In the seminar we've humorously and honestly shared mistakes we've personally made—simply from the experience of having been there, done that—while video clips from celebrity couples incorporate their counsel.

Many marriage manuals and courses teach people what *to* do in marriage while fewer expound on what *not* to do. Inasmuch as we've both had plenty of experience in making marital missteps, we felt fairly well qualified to be reporters of this sort of wisdom.

We developed "Six Steps to a Successful Relationship." To help you remember, once the elements are all put together, they spell out L-A-U-G-H-S.

As you read through these six steps, try sizing up your own marriage or relationship against them. If you're dating someone, use these six steps as a yardstick to see if he or she measures up to you.

LAUGHTER

We can learn a few things about laughter from children.

Kids smile or laugh four hundred times a day.

We adults? We smile or laugh fifteen times per day. Uh-oh. What does that tell us?

We've learned from interviewing scores of happily married couples that laughter is a key ingredient to their success.

Laughter is the perfect tool for you or your spouse to employ when a conversation starts getting tense and has the earmarks of elevating into a full-blown argument. When you crack a joke or start making fun of yourself with a funny face or voice, humor will almost always let the steam out of the moment.

> YOU CAN TURN PAINFUL SITUATIONS
> AROUND THROUGH LAUGHTER. IF YOU CAN
> FIND HUMOR IN ANYTHING, EVEN POVERTY,
> YOU CAN SURVIVE IT.[1]
>
> —BILL COSBY

SILLY LITTLE GREEN FROGGY

Linda was miffed.

"This *therapeutic separation* isn't working very well," she sputtered, cleaning up the mess in the guest bathroom—capping the toothpaste and rinsing off the grimy bar of soap Glen left on the counter instead of the soap dish.

"This is so typical of our thoughtless marriage," she said, forcefully tossing loose tissues and an empty shampoo bottle into an overflowing trash can. "Thirty-nine years of it."

As part of their therapeutic separation, Glen had moved into an RV parked at a campsite down the road. He was permitted to come into the house while Linda was at work, to take a shower and do his laundry.

"Why can't he clean up after himself," she grumbled.

It was good Glen wasn't there. She would have given him a piece of her mind.

What happened to that man I fell in love with as a teenager back in Iowa? He used to make me laugh. Now all he does is make me mad.

The spark had fizzled from their marriage like a slow leak in an old inner tube. After the kids had grown up and moved out, they were just two resentful people living under the same roof. Finally, Linda had had enough. She asked for a divorce.

Glen argued he didn't want one. He convinced her, instead, to try going to a couples therapist, which they'd been doing every week for ninety minutes. It was the therapist who recommended the therapeutic separation, but there was no evidence it was doing any good. Every session with the therapist seemed to be a rehash of what "he did," "she did," or either of them "didn't do." Their communication was cold, indifferent, or cranky.

Linda moved on to her own bathroom to begin tidying up.

Pulling back the shower curtain, her state of mind instantly changed. A tight-lipped sentimental smile came over her face as she reached for her young granddaughter's green bathtub toy, Froggy, left behind from her last visit.

Linda fondly picked it up, not quite knowing where to put it.

A mischievous thought surged into her mind. *I'll put this silly little green frog in Glen's bathroom. Maybe it'll scare him into princely behavior.*

Carefully she propped the little frog, staring upward, atop the toilet brush.

With a self-satisfied smile, she went on with her work.

"The next afternoon I went into my bathroom," says Linda. "And there he sat on the edge of the toilet seat. Froggy. I burst out laughing."

When she went into Glen's bathroom she was astonished. "It positively sparkled.

Toothpaste, comb, and deodorant put away, the tub spotless—victory!

Quickly she calculated that Glen would be coming the next day to do his laundry.

"I had the perfect spot for Froggy: on top of the agitator in the washer. A sort of *thank you* gesture," she said.

Then two days later, Linda opened her medicine cabinet, and there he was, the silly little frog staring her in the face.

She giggled, plopping Froggy on the bar of soap in Glen's shower.

"How are things going?" asked the therapist at their next session.

"Well," said Glen, glancing at Linda, "actually we've been hiding this frog around . . ."

Linda and Glen couldn't control themselves. They started laughing. And in between giggles, they explained the mysterious travels of the silly little green frog from one place to the next.

The therapist looked pleased. "Perhaps you're ready to start dating," she said matter-of-factly.

"Dating?" asked Linda, her face feeling flushed.

During the therapist session they made a plan to go to a flea market, agreeing not to discuss their relationship.

When Linda later telephoned her daughter Karen about the impending *date*, her offspring followed up with another question: "What are you wearing, Mom?"

Linda hadn't thought about that.

"Mom, you need to look cute for Dad," added Karen.

Linda picked out a new outfit at Nordstrom's Last Chance department. Considering that this was a last-chance mission for her marriage, she fleetingly wondered, *Is that a godwink?*

When Glen arrived at the front door for their date, he was smartly dressed, handsomely groomed, and holding a bouquet of flowers.

"I found that I was as awkward as a wife as Glen was as a husband," she said later.

The flea-market date graduated to dinner and then to chatting about the kids.

"Karen told me to bring flowers," said Glen, grinning sheepishly. They laughed as they talked about their "conniving matchmaker."

"Should we do this again?" asked Glen as he walked Linda to the front door.

Holding each other's hands, Linda said, "Absolutely!"

A few weeks later, Linda and Glen were ready to recommit to their relationship, bolstered by a technique they had learned in the therapy sessions: praying together. And just to help keep them focused . . . and laughing . . . silly little green Froggy still shows up from place to place, time to time.[2]

"When you lose the fun of life, you lose a strong component of who you are," reflects Linda. "That little frog made a big turn-around in my life. And we laughed ourselves silly."

"I have never felt better about our relationship," she confides. "Glen feels the same. Our intimate life is better . . . our social life is better . . . everything."

She describes her own "180 degree" attitudinal change with this illustration: "Glen used to say, 'Would you like to go to Home Depot?' I'd think, *Why in the dickens would I want to go to Home Depot?* Now when he asks, I say, 'Oh yeah! I'll be there in three seconds!'"

GOOD CHEER IS OFFICIALLY THERAPEUTIC

The Bible says that a cheerful heart does the body good (Proverbs 17:22). The medical profession agrees with that. It's finding amazing benefits to laughter, such as an elvaluation in your immune system and the release of those feel-good hormones.

This thesis was made known by former *Saturday Review* editor Norman Cousins, whose personal medical experiences led to the book *Anatomy of an Illness as Perceived by the Patient.*

Cousins suffered from a collagen illness, which doctors suspected was caused by exposure to heavy-metal poisoning.

Medical treatment called for heavy doses of painkillers that Cousins concluded also carried harmful side effects.

Delving into more research, Cousins determined that negative and positive emotions had a distinct effect on recovery. He therefore prescribed a radical course of treatment: laughter. He had his nurse read him funny stories in between Marx Brothers movies. The more he laughed, the better he got, until he was able to withdraw himself from all painkillers.

Eventually, the *Journal of the American Medical Association* embraced Cousins' thesis in a 1989 article.[3]

Mark Stibich, PhD, writing on longevity for About.com, says Norwegian researchers, studying 54,000 people over seven years, indicated that laughter can extend life.

"Those that found the world the most funny were 35 percent less likely to die during the study period," writes Stibich. "A person . . . diagnosed with cancer . . . was 70 times more likely to survive . . . if laughter and humor [were] an important part of his . . . life."[4]

So laugh a lot. It will improve your health and lengthen your life.

APPRECIATION

It's human nature to want to be around people who want to be around you. Friends make us feel good about ourselves when they build up our self-esteem.

Recall the smile that breaks out on your face when someone says, "Hey, you look great in that color," or when they acknowledge something positive you've done. "You were so right when you said ..." or "I don't know where you got the courage to do ..."

Why, then, isn't it as easy to show appreciation for your husband's or wife's traits or actions on a daily basis?

If your wife has a knack for decorating, tell her. Again and again. If she looks great in that blue dress, tell her how beautiful she is.

If your husband is a great father, tell him how wonderful he is with the kids. If he has a cute smile, tell him. Even if it's for the one hundredth time.

Find ways to express appreciation for each other several times every day. And when you can, praise your spouse in front of others.

Also remember to do little thoughtful things for each other, such as opening the door for her or sticking thoughtful notes in his briefcase.

Respect and value each other's opinion.

Be affectionate in public.

Never let the sun set without expressing appreciation for things—even the very smallest things—that your partner has done to make your day better.

In the following story, Mary Ellen and Jimi, one of our couples in The 40 Day Prayer Challenge, demonstrate how appreciation can be conveyed through praise.

TELL ME A STORY

The first time we met Jimi, he reminded us of a comic-strip character ... massively muscular with a sweetness of personality.

On a construction site, Jimi can heft a bundle of building

materials in the manner many of us might lift a few fireplace logs. His blond hair, spiking from the sweatband that circles his brow, frames a face that lights up, almost shyly, when he talks about Mary Ellen. You know right then and there that this body that could have belonged to Arnold Schwarzenegger has a heart that came from a teddy bear.

"Mary Ellen has changed my life," he says with twinkling eyes and a grin. "I never prayed with someone . . . but praying with her has given me courage . . . the two of us talking with God, a third person that we can't physically see."

Jimi and Mary Ellen, both single for several years and comfortable with independent lifestyles, began their engagement with daily prayer, simultaneously participating in The 40 Day Prayer Challenge.

Mary Ellen, very attractive and slim, speaks with quiet strength and a mother's heart. "We pray for maybe five minutes every morning or evening or both," she says.

As a unique and pleasurable conclusion to their daily prayer time, Mary Ellen has encouraged the use of storytelling to express appreciation to Jimi. "I ask Jimi to read me stories," she says, "and I find it very comforting. It reminds me of when I was a child and someone I loved read to me. Now, it's very romantic."

Jimi's face lights up as he rejoins: "When Mary Ellen first asked me to read to her, I felt proud. Clearing my throat and sitting a little taller, I said, 'Really, you want me to read to you?' I mean, what an honor."

"He picks out something uplifting—a story you'd want to have on your mind just before falling asleep," says Mary Ellen.

"Then the other day, she surprised me; she asked me to *tell* her a story. I had to think about that for a moment; then I picked up the happy sound of the birds. So I told her that the sound of birds chirping reminded me of something I really looked forward to when I was a boy—I described getting up at sunrise with my dad, packing things to go fishing. All those birds were happy as could be, and so was I."

"That's how you learn about someone," says Mary Ellen, "when he tells you a story."

Jimi's body shifts slightly in the chair, as his head bows. Then his entire frame lifts, a signal that he is about to share something more personal. "When she asks me to tell or read her a story, it shows me that she loves me. Appreciates me. It's very intimate."

Writer Alan Cohen puts it nicely: "Appreciation is the highest form of prayer, for it acknowledges the presence of good wherever you shine the light of your thankful thoughts."[5]

UNDERSTAND

"You never listen to me."

The person who says that really means: "You may be listening with your ears . . . you may hear me, technically . . . but you aren't *understanding* what I am trying to tell you."

Janice and Jeff had challenges in that area. Jeff had a tendency to dismiss what Janice was saying. Janice would then shut down. She didn't feel safe in expressing her feelings.

We all have a need to be understood and validated.

Most women are more sensitive when it comes to being heard. They need to be handled with care. The most loving thing a man can do for his wife is to be still and listen; to avoid analysis, criticism, or interruptions—the innate male reaction is a desire to fix the situation. There is much wisdom in the Scriptures on this topic. It's summed up with: "Everyone should be quick to listen, slow to speak" (James 1:19).

One method that seems to work well for couples is to develop the habit of repeating what your partner has just said, in different words, showing that you're really hearing *and* understanding.

In conversation, be attentive. Use body language to show that you're engaged in the dialog, not distracted, uninterested, or impatient.

Your spouse needs to feel free to articulate her feelings. So let her know that you want to know her concerns.

A college basketball coach with one of the greatest winning streaks of all time, Coach John Wooden of UCLA, once said, "Marriage requires that each partner listen to the other side. It's like what I say about leadership. 'You must be interested in finding the *best* way, not in having your *own* way.'"[6]

GOD

God is at the center of the L-A-U-G-H-S acronym. God should also be in the center of your relationship.

If you want balance in your marriage then give Him His rightful place. Let Him be your family therapist. Surely the best marriage manual ever written is the Word of God. Every question you have is answered there. It's your insurance policy for a long and wonderful life.

All too often marriage failure is blamed on communication

problems, personality clashes, financial difficulties, or not having enough time to tend to the relationship. Those problems diminish when you pray together regularly as a couple.

Our couples in this book are representative of men and women who are discovering the extraordinary, life-changing benefits of daily prayer together. If you place God at the center of your relationship, we guarantee that your marriage will be happier; you'll have fewer arguments, better communication, and more respect for each other, and your lovemaking will be more fulfilling. It's simple. Couples who pray together, stay together. Don't leave God outside the marriage covenant. Open the door and let Him in. He has the keys to release incredible blessings into your life. Spend quality time, every day, with the greatest of all counselors. You have His undivided attention. The more love and respect you give to God and your spouse, the more you get back in return. It will be like putting money in a love bank. It's the best investment you can make.

HONOR

THE BEST THING A MAN CAN DO FOR HIS CHILDREN IS TO LOVE THEIR MOTHER.[7]

—ABRAHAM LINCOLN

When a couple recites its marriage vows, often you'll hear the words *to have and to hold*. But what does that really mean?

It means to hold up your spouse . . . above yourself. To love and to honor your life's companion.

How do you do that?

Don't take your husband or wife for granted. Make your mate your priority. That is God's divine order. The husband and wife should take precedence over everything else. That includes career, family, friends, and children.

Yes, children.

One of the biggest mistakes couples make is to allow the children to enter into that sacred place that belongs to you, your spouse, and God.

It may seem logical that a child needs more attention, so as a parent you feel as though you need to tend to the *squeaky wheel*. When that happens, before you know it, your spouse is on the back burner, and all your energy is going to the kids.

Strong, successful marriages have demonstrated over and over that the best thing you can do for your children is to constantly demonstrate that your marriage is a fortress. This can be done by praying as a couple in front of the children and with the children.

Never fall for the temptation to give your all to the kids.

Think of your marriage as the circles on a dartboard. In the bull's-eye there is room for only three. You, your spouse, and God.

Children belong in the second ring.

Other family members belong in the third ring and so on.

There's good reason why the Bible says that when you get married you become *one flesh*. It means your hearts are joined together.

Your children will feel the security of parents who radiate the power of love, who are shielded by the power of prayer.

Support

"I've got your back!"

Isn't that the message—spoken or unspoken—you always want to hear from your partner?

To be able to trust in the support of your partner, no matter what, is crucial in the success of your relationship. You have to feel safe discussing your concerns, your dreams, and your desires. And you need to know that your partner is a willing ally in helping you to achieve everything you want.

When you place your plans before God in daily prayer, asking for His guidance and discernment, you will begin to feel that spousal support, more and more.

Most of us will never be called upon to demonstrate the level of support that Ken exemplifies for Cathy in the following story, but it surely is a wonderful model.

Why, Oh, Why?

Our dear friends Cathy and Ken Campbell were celebrating the time of their lives. They were spending a week in the idyllic country-side of Maine—biking, walking, shopping, and dining. They were on a much-needed vacation, enjoying the new pleasures of retirement.

After a decade of growing a small church on the island of Martha's Vineyard off the coast of Massachusetts, they made the tough decision to finally utter that word: *retire*. It was a bitter-sweet Sunday when Pastor Ken gave his last sermon and Cathy played her final hymn on the piano. Ken's teachings were always compelling, and Cathy's effervescent, engaging personality made you feel that all was right with the world.

Ken never once had regretted leaving his thirty-year career with IBM to become a small-town pastor. He went from working nine to five to 24/7. But he loved tending his flock. His door was always open to anyone who needed prayer, counseling, or just a good cup of coffee.

But there came a time when Ken and Cathy knew God was leading them down new paths, in search of new horizons. Ken's studies for a doctorate in ministry germinated fresh ideas in his mind, and a promising offer to teach young pastors had come his way. Meanwhile, Cathy was hitting her stride in a new home-based entrepreneurial business.

It was a new season and they were excited about all the possibilities that God had in store for them.

Then, in an instant, their dreams were shattered.

Cathy and Ken were biking on a country road through Acadia National Park. Coasting downhill just behind Ken, Cathy suddenly lost control of her bike and slammed into a tree. She was catapulted backward and struck a rock.

"Ken," she shouted stoically, "I can't feel my legs!"

She couldn't move.

Within ten minutes emergency medical technicians responded to Ken's 9-1-1 call. Cathy was transported by helicopter to the trauma center at Eastern Maine Medical Center. Following surgery and two weeks in intensive care, she was airlifted to a facility in Atlanta that specializes in spinal cord injuries.

The verdict: Cathy had fractured her T-5 vertebra and bruised her spinal cord. She was paralyzed from the rib cage down.

She would never walk again.

Cathy and Ken's lives were turned upside down. Abandoning established routines to plan ahead, they were consumed with pain management and getting through one day at a time. Instead of talking with friends, they were barely able to read the messages that poured in to them on a Web site called Caringbridge.

Cathy had always been a doer. Now she could do very little. And when she did, it was painful. Everything, it seemed, required assistance. And Ken became her full-time caregiver. He also became an expert on Cathy's particular spinal cord injury. He studied everything he could in order to give her the best possible care.

One of the most difficult things for Cathy to get used to was not being able to control bodily functions. Several times during the day and night, Ken would have to catheterize her. He carried her into and out of her wheelchair and lifted her into and out of the car to drive her to therapy sessions.

Until she could learn to manage some things on her own, Cathy was totally dependent upon Ken.

Yet never did anyone hear words of complaint uttered by either of them.

They replaced the average intimacies of marriage with more intimate prayer times with God.

Someone asked Cathy, "Why did God allow this to happen to you?"

"Why not?" she bubbled. "We don't know how, right now, but this, too, is for His glory."

Every day they pray that God will direct them to a new ministry. They don't know what it is yet. But they know it will come.

Cathy knows she has to get herself in shape to accept the new calling. She has to be strong. Perhaps that's why, ten months after her accident, she was determined to propel her wheelchair the entire three-mile route of the annual Martha's Vineyard Fourth of July parade.

As crowds at every turn cheered her on, the sign on the back of Cathy's wheelchair expressed her gratitude: Thanks for Your Prayers.

Cathy and Ken continue to have good days and bad days. They feel challenged but never defeated. One evening, months after her injury, Cathy had a toileting accident. As Ken was tending to her, her eyes filled with tears.

She cried out, "Ken, could you have ever imagined that one day you would be doing this for me?"

Ken looked up to her with a love that welled from deep within. Softly, he said, "Cathy . . . I consider it a privilege."

⚘

CATHY'S INJURY is not something either of them would have chosen, but they know God is sovereign, and they trust that He knew what He was doing that day in Maine.

They also know they have a choice.

They could complain about their condition. Or—as they have chosen—they can thank God for whatever He has planned.

They could cloak themselves in self-pity. Or—as they have chosen—they can model commitment and determination for the rest of us.

Cathy and Ken Campbell, better than anyone we know, have taken that oft-uttered plea, "Why did you do this to me, God?" and changed but one word: "Why did you do this *for* me, God?"

SUPPORT IS WORKING TOGETHER AS A TEAM

I CAN DO ALL THINGS
THROUGH CHRIST, BECAUSE HE
GIVES ME STRENGTH.

—PHILIPPIANS 4:13 NCV

If you and your partner work as a team, you can create possibilities you could never have done alone. Remember the 1980 U.S. hockey team that won the Olympic gold medal against all odds? They won because each player supported the others. They all had the same goal. And they all believed they could reach it.

The media called them *the dream team.*

You can make your marriage the dream team too. Let God be your coach. He will help you press toward your goal.

Our job as a husband and wife is to gird each other up, to support each other's dream, and to trust God to direct us on a wonderful journey.

PUT THE SIX STEPS ALL TOGETHER

We've had the pleasure of watching couples—some married a long time, others newly married—apply these six steps into their daily lives as a habit. When you do, along with a regimen of joint daily prayer, success will always follow. And you'll have lots of *laughs*.

Once again, the Six Steps to a Successful Relationship are:

L   Laughter
A   Appreciation
U   Understanding
G   God
H   Honor
S   Support

OUTCOMES

If you and your partner have not already begun your participation in The 40 Day Prayer Challenge, we hope we've given you enough incentive to do so.

The vast majority of our pilot group of twenty-four couples stuck with it, committing to a minimum of five minutes of daily prayer. And we understand—finding that five minutes for the two of you to do anything together is not always easy.

Nonetheless, our couples saw amazing results. They found that prayer had a soothing effect overall. They said praying together was "liberating and powerful." They also noticed an increase in heartfelt conversation. Respect for each other rose to new heights.

Conflicts were resolved quicker and easier, and lovemaking was more freeing and fulfilling.

When couples placed God at the center of their marriage, they changed their behavior and became more empathetic toward each other. They saw each other as the protector, not as the victim, creating strong feelings of love and appreciation.

You can get all the support you will need during The 40 Day Prayer Challenge, including weekly notes of encouragement from the two of us and access to many other resources, such as a fun-filled yet life-changing Friday night and Saturday morning workshop entitled Pray Together, Stay Together.

Just Starting?

If you decided to finish reading this book before making a commitment to pray together five minutes a day for forty days, here's a reminder on how to get started.

First, sit down and together fill out the initial questionnaire found in appendix 1. Or get on your computer and go to www.coupleswhopray.com. There you can sign up and fill out the questionnaire prepared by Baylor University's Institute for Studies of Religion that will help you track your own progress, from beginning to end.

For about the price of a designer cup of coffee and a bagel, you can get all the support you'll need during The 40 Day Prayer Challenge—weekly notes of encouragement from the two of us and access to many other resources, including a one-hour presentation called "Couples Who Pray Live!" filled with romance, inspiration, and comedy.

Another advantage to the online version of the challenge is that you can compare your own scores on marital progress with the national average.

Parenting Prayer

It has been very evident that prayer is a powerful mortar for a marriage. But prayer also helps build a strong foundation for your children.

Denzel Washington's wife, Pauletta, discussed with us the positive influences of seeing her own parents openly praying together as she grew up.

Donna Summer had a similar experience. "I grew up watching my mother and father pray. We prayed in our house or in public, whether anybody watched or not."

She and her husband, Bruce Sudano, continued that habit when they became parents. "Our children have witnessed us praying together all their lives," says Bruce.

Donna elaborates: "From the time our children were little, my husband and I would put them to bed and whisper affirmations of God in their ear as they would go to sleep. We would tell them how wonderful they were as people, how loved they were, and that everyone loved them and that God would always love them. I can see the difference in my children by having those affirmations. It's just powerful . . . prayer is powerful stuff."

Perhaps you will want to follow these examples—in addition to your private prayer time, to pray in front of your children and to include them in family prayer.

Great marriages have a trickle-down effect on children. When parents speak and act lovingly toward each other, kids pattern that behavior. When God takes residence in your home, it makes for a much calmer household. You'll find that there is a divine order to even the smallest of daily tasks.

LET GOD BE YOUR WEDDING PLANNER

Not long ago we drove by a little church with a great saying posted out front: "Loved the wedding, invite me to the marriage! God."

A friend of ours, Bill Banuchi, puts it this way: "The wedding takes an hour. The marriage takes a lifetime."

The world has taken weddings to a whole new place. The emphasis is on the dress, the flowers, the cake, the invited guests. It's more like a Broadway opening than a sacred event.

How do we make sure that more marriages last?

Change the mind-set. Stop focusing on the wedding and focus on the marriage.

If you are just beginning a life together with someone, this is when you need to start bringing God into the relationship.

As Rick Warren once said in a *Living the Life* TV interview, "Almost everything in life has an instruction booklet. Your microwave has one. Your toaster has one. So do you. It's called the Bible."

Just follow the directions. Our manufacturer has figured everything out for us. If we follow His design, the foundation for our marriage won't crumble but will grow stronger and stronger. Think of your spouse as part of your body. If you harm him or her, you're really harming the both of you.

Here is a confirmation from the instruction manual:

Though one may be overpowered, two can defend themselves. A cord of three strands is not quickly broken.
—Ecclesiastes 4:12

WORD OF CAUTION

As our friend Samantha Landy—author of *Savvy Singles*—reminds
us, "Use extreme caution when praying together with someone who
is not yet your spouse."

Because prayer is, indeed, the most intimate act between a
man and a woman, the very act of praying together can be highly
combustible.

Or, as in the case of the following story, prayer can come to
the rescue.

A SINGLE WOMAN'S FORTRESS

"I prayed for you and your project last night," said Luci.

"Nobody prays for me," replied the man with an air of charm.

Luci Swindoll was a vibrant, creative single woman, mid-
fortyish and comfortable with her single status. She enjoyed her
own space in her small apartment near Dallas. She had a busy
schedule as a part-time opera singer, which somehow fit into her
full-time schedule as an artist for Mobil Oil Corporation where
she transformed the engineering ideas in the minds of PhDs into
something tangible for them and others to see. "I pray for a lot of
people," continued Luci with a wide smile and a short laugh.

She was talking with a Frenchman who was in America on a temporary visa with his wife and children. He was one of those PhDs, drawn to the office of this beautiful woman with an outgoing personality and something else—a certain light about her that no one could explain.

"You really believe this stuff?" he playfully challenged.

"I could show you the scriptures to back it up," said Luci confidently. She looked at her watch. "Gotta go. I have an opera rehearsal," she said, starting to put her things away.

"You're a singer?"

"Yes, I sing in Dallas. You should come. Bring your wife. My mother and father will be there. And maybe my brother . . . he's a well-known minister . . . Chuck Swindoll."

That weekend the man from France did show up at the opera. But without his wife. That should have been Luci's first warning sign. After the performance, he sought her out, and she felt she ought to invite her colleague to the restaurant along with her parents.

"What are your hobbies?" inquired the man as they dined, demonstrating a continued interest in Luci.

"I'm working on a ship . . . I build little model ships," said Luci with a smile.

"May I come by and see it?" he asked, again showing genuine interest in her work.

"I'm not really comfortable with that," said Luci.

"Why not?"

"Well, primarily because I have too much to do this afternoon to have anybody over," she added.

"Oh, I'd just stop by and take a look at your ship—just a

moment or two. In fact, what's your phone number? I'll call my wife and let her know where I am."

"All right," said Luci in a reluctant tone, only slightly more assured. All the way home she prayed about the uneasiness she felt about this guy dropping in because she lived alone and doubted his motive. "God, I ask You to guide me. Please keep me safe, Lord."

"May I have a cup of coffee?" said the man as he walked in the door.

Luci began to fix the coffee.

In his disarmingly charming manner and French accent, he complimented her skills in building the model ship.

Then the man began his moves. For the next several minutes Luci was in a constant struggle to thwart his attempts to pull her to him, to kiss her. He was strong, insistent, and committed to his goal.

"Stop that!" demanded Luci. "Sit down." Her strong voice belied the terror she felt on the inside. *How did I let myself into this situation . . . alone in my apartment with this man and his frightening intentions?*

She sat down. He sat right beside her.

"You need to sit over there, across from me." She pointed, her heart now racing. "With my contacts, I can't see you very well unless you're in front of me."

As the man took the seat across from her, he began to take a different tactic.

"In London I had nine girlfriends," he said. "What do you think of that?"

Luci simply looked at him. *How can I end this . . . yet allow my colleague to retain his dignity?* She wondered. *I don't want to be rude; I just want him to leave me alone.*

"I would like to do something very intimate with you," he continued softly, his accent making the word *intimate* more seductive.

"I know what you want. I'm not doing that," said Luci. "But I will do something intimate with you." She paused for just a beat. "The most intimate thing a man and a woman can do . . . I'll pray with you."

He looked at her. For what seemed like a minute, the man studied Luci's firm countenance . . . taking in what she had just said.

"I want us to pray together," she said, finally.

"How do you do that?"

"We talk to God . . . just the way we're talking here."

"I don't know how to do that. Would you start?"

"Yes."

"Do I have to pray out loud?"

"No, if you like, you can just listen . . . but if you wish to speak, you can."

Luci began to pray. "Heavenly Father, I love You. I confess, Father, that what is on the mind of the man who is with me makes me uncomfortable. But I pray for him, Lord, for his wife, and his children . . ."

As she completed her prayer, three or four minutes later, Luci squinted through closed eyes. The man's head was bowed. His hands clasped. Then, hearing him actually speak surprised her.

"God, I know You don't know the sound of my voice, but You know Luci's . . . and I pray that You would do whatever You do to help me know You better."

At the end of his prayer the man looked at Luci and said, "You know . . . that's the first time I ever talked to God."

"How did it feel?" asked Luci.

"You were right. It's a very intimate experience."

At that moment the phone rang. It was the man's wife.

What do you know? He did *give her my number*, she thought, handing him the phone.

"Yes, darling, I'm on my way right now," he said.

Whew.

⚜

TWO YEARS LATER, Luci saw the man again.

"I've thought many times about the day we prayed," he said. "You remained a dignified woman and never put me down. I want to thank you for that."

"Do you believe in God yet? Have you talked to Him anymore?" she asked with a smile.

He nodded. "No, I haven't talked to Him anymore, but I do think about Him and wonder what He's really like."

⚜

TODAY LUCI SWINDOLL has put her full-time opera singing and drawing career in the past. She spends nearly three dozen weeks a year traveling to huge arenas in cities across the country as one of the founding members and outstanding speakers of Women of Faith®.

THANKS FOR TUNING IN

As television people, we've learned to be grateful that we've retained someone's attention all the way to the end of a program.

We are all the more gratified that you are reading these words now, suggesting that you've read this entire book. For we consider this to be one of the most important opportunities we have ever had to communicate deeply heartfelt thoughts to you.

We pray that the stories have inspired you to take the journey—The 40 Day Prayer Challenge—to a happier and more gratifying life.

You don't have to hope that someday things will change in your marriage. *Happily ever after* doesn't have to be just in fairy tales. It can become a reality you can begin today.

Wisdom from the Scriptures tells us that "the fruit of the Spirit is love, joy, [and] peace" (Gal. 5:22).

The fruit is there for the picking. But you have to reach for it. Take it. When you do, God will bless you with rich rewards that no amount of money can buy.

Our wish is that you will take the steps that will infuse your marriage with the love, peace, and joy that God wants you to have. His desire is to create a wonderful life for you. You truly can have a match made in heaven. You just need to ask Him. By praying together.

—Louise and SQuire

APPENDIX 1

COUPLES WHO PRAY:
THE MOST INTIMATE ACT BETWEEN A
MAN AND A WOMAN

INITIAL QUESTIONNAIRE

Prepared with the
Institute for Studies of Religion
Baylor University

These questions will help you begin The 40 Day Prayer Challenge,
a commitment to pray together on a daily basis for a minimum
of five minutes a day at a suitable time and place.

The mission of the Couples Who Pray Initial Questionnaire
is to help you measure the outcome of prayer—distinct and positive outcomes for your marriage.

Two identical surveys follow, one labeled for the husband the
other designated for the wife.

APPENDIX 1

At the end of your forty days, revisit this questionnaire, comparing your original answers with how you answer them at that time.

Have fun. And get ready for a life-changing experience.

166

Husband's Survey

1. Your age: _____

2. How long have you been in your present marriage?
   a) ___ Less than 5 years
   b) ___ Less than 10 years
   c) ___ Less than 15 years
   d) ___ 15 years or more

3. Is this your first marriage?
   a) ___ Yes
   b) ___ No, this is my second marriage.
   c) ___ No, this is my third marriage or more.

4. Do you and your wife currently pray together?
   a) ___ Almost daily
   b) ___ Sometimes
   c) ___ Rarely
   d) ___ Never
   [If you indicated "Never," skip to question 12]

5. If so, for how long?
   a) ___ 5–10 minutes
   b) ___ 15–30 minutes
   c) ___ 30–45 minutes
   d) ___ 45–60 minutes

6. Do you have a special place to pray?
  a) ____ Yes. Where? _____
  b) ____ No

7. Do you have a favorite time of the day to pray?
  a) ____ First thing in the morning
  b) ____ During the day
  c) ____ Around dinnertime
  d) ____ Before bedtime

8. Do you pray aloud with each other?
  a) ____ Yes
  b) ____ No, silently

9. Does one partner generally speak during prayer?
  a) ____ Yes, while the other partner generally listens.
  b) ____ No, we both speak.

10. Do you generally pray together at mealtimes?
  a) ____ Yes
  b) ____ No

11. Do you pray together at times of hardship or crisis?
  a) ____ Yes
  b) ____ No

12. Have you thought about praying together but just didn't know how to get started?

    a) ___ Yes.

    b) ___ No, praying together never crossed our minds.

13. In prayer, do you ask God for specific things you want to happen in your personal and family lives?

    a) ___ Yes.

    b) ___ No, we usually pray only for others.

14. Do you feel you have the right to ask God for personal gifts or blessings?

    a) ___ Yes.

    b) ___ No, we were not brought up that way.

15. Do you express gratitude in prayer, thanking God for blessings?

    a) ___ Always

    b) ___ Sometimes

    c) ___ Rarely

    d) ___ Never

16. Do you and your wife read the Bible together as a part of your prayer time?

    a) ___ Yes

    b) ___ No, not normally

    c) ___ Yes, but at times other than prayer time

17. All things considered, would you say *your life* these days is
  a) ___ Very happy
  b) ___ Somewhat happy
  c) ___ Not too happy

18. All things considered *in your marriage*, would you say things these days are
  a) ___ Very happy
  b) ___ Somewhat happy
  c) ___ Not too happy

19. Many people think marriages go through cycles, over and over again. If so, where would you place your marriage at the present time?
  a) ___ Falling in love
  b) ___ Settling down
  c) ___ Bottoming out
  d) ___ Beginning again

20. Considering that most couples sometimes argue, in an average week, how often would you say that cross words are spoken?
  a) ___ Every day
  b) ___ Three to five times a week
  c) ___ A few times a month
  d) ___ Rarely
  e) ___ Never

21. Do you feel that you and your wife are able to chat with each other as frequently as you would like?

    a) ___ Yes.

    b) ___ No, we need to make more time for conversation.

22. In an average day, how many conversations do you imagine you have with each other?

    a) ___ One or two times

    b) ___ Several times

    c) ___ A lot

23. What would be a rough estimate of the total minutes you converse with your wife during an average day?

    a) ___ 5–10 minutes

    b) ___ 15–30 minutes

    c) ___ 60 minutes or more

24. How many times *a month* do you and your wife make love?

    a) ___ Rarely, if ever

    b) ___ One time or less

    c) ___ Generally less than four times

    d) ___ Probably an average of five to ten times

    e) ___ More

25. Which of the following best describes your feelings about the frequency of your lovemaking?

    a) ___ I would like lovemaking to be more frequent.

    b) ___ It's fine now.

    c) ___ Just not interested.

26. Which describes the level of satisfaction you feel with love-making?

    a) ___ Would like it to be more satisfying.

    b) ___ It is just fine now.

27. Do you agree that there's a correlation between lovemaking and prayer?

    a) ___ I doubt it.

    b) ___ Possibly, but I'm not certain.

    c) ___ I agree, mildly.

    d) ___ I agree, strongly.

28. On a scale of 1 to 10, where would you currently rank your *marital happiness*?

    (1 = very unhappy; 10 = very happy) _____

29. How often do you and your spouse do the following?

A lot	Sometimes	Rarely	Never	No answer
1	2	3	4	5

a) Hold hands

1	2	3	4	5

b) Laugh together

1	2	3	4	5

c) Go for walks, biking, golf, or other activities

1	2	3	4	5

d) Touch each other fondly

    1   2   3   4   5

e) Rub each other's back or feet

    1   2   3   4   5

f) Enjoy romantic dates together

    1   2   3   4   5

g) Leave love notes to each other

    1   2   3   4   5

h) Go to parties together

    1   2   3   4   5

i) Enjoy the same music and movies together

    1   2   3   4   5

j) Talk privately and lovingly to one another

    1   2   3   4   5

k) Ask about each other's work and activities

    1   2   3   4   5

l) Go to religious services together

    1   2   3   4   5

m) Honor each other respectfully

    1   2   3   4   5

n) Really try to understand each other's feelings

| 1 | 2 | 3 | 4 | 5 |

o) Protect your marriage by watching each other's back

| 1 | 2 | 3 | 4 | 5 |

30. Considering where your marriage is right now, where would you rank your fear of divorce?
- a) ___ 50/50
- b) ___ 25 percent or so
- c) ___ 10 percent or so
- d) ___ 1 percent or less

31. Some husbands like to have guys' night out. Is that something that appeals to you?
- a) ___ Appeals to me a lot.
- b) ___ Occasionally, it's fun.
- c) ___ Rarely, I'd rather be with my spouse.

32. Which answer best describes how you consider your marriage?
- a) ___ A married couple doing our best to keep it together
- b) ___ Pretty good companions most of the time
- c) ___ Best friends with a strong foundation

33. Which best describes your experience with your church or religious organization?

a) ___ We have received little or no encouragement to pray with each other.

b) ___ We have heard just a little about praying together.

c) ___ We have heard some encouragement about this topic.

d) ___ There has been strong emphasis and encouragement for couples to pray together.

Wife's Survey

1. Your age: _____

2. How long have you been in your present marriage?
   a) ____ Less than 5 years
   b) ____ Less than 10 years
   c) ____ Less than 15 years
   d) ____ 15 years or more

3. Is this your first marriage?
   a) ____ Yes
   b) ____ No, this is my second marriage.
   c) ____ No, this is my third marriage or more.

4. Do you and your husband currently pray together?
   a) ____ Almost daily
   b) ____ Sometimes
   c) ____ Rarely
   d) ____ Never
   [If you indicated "Never," skip to question 12]

5. If so, for how long?
   a) ____ 5–10 minutes
   b) ____ 15–30 minutes
   c) ____ 30–45 minutes
   d) ____ 45–60 minutes

6. Do you have a special place to pray?

    a) ___ Yes. Where? _____

    b) ___ No

7. Do you have a favorite time of the day to pray?

    a) ___ First thing in the morning

    b) ___ During the day

    c) ___ Around dinnertime

    d) ___ Before bedtime

8. Do you pray aloud with each other?

    a) ___ Yes

    b) ___ No, silently

9. Does one partner generally speak during prayer?

    a) ___ Yes, while the other partner generally listens.

    b) ___ No, we both speak.

10. Do you generally pray together at mealtimes?

    a) ___ Yes

    b) ___ No

11. Do you pray together at times of hardship or crisis?

    a) ___ Yes

    b) ___ No

12. Have you thought about praying together but just didn't know how to get started?

    a) ___ Yes.

    b) ___ No, praying together never crossed our minds.

13. In prayer, do you ask God for specific things you want to happen in your personal and family lives?

    a) ___ Yes.

    b) ___ No, we usually pray only for others.

14. Do you feel you have the right to ask God for personal gifts or blessings?

    a) ___ Yes.

    b) ___ No, we were not brought up that way.

15. Do you express gratitude in prayer, thanking God for blessings?

    a) ___ Always

    b) ___ Sometimes

    c) ___ Rarely

    d) ___ Never

16. Do you and your husband read the Bible together as a part of your prayer time?

    a) ___ Yes

    b) ___ No, not normally

    c) ___ Yes, but at times other than prayer time

17. All things considered, would you say *your life* these days is
 a) ___ Very happy
 b) ___ Somewhat happy
 c) ___ Not too happy

18. All things considered *in your marriage*, would you say things these days are
 a) ___ Very happy
 b) ___ Somewhat happy
 c) ___ Not too happy

19. Many people think marriages go through cycles, over and over again. If so, where would you place your marriage at the present time?
 a) ___ Falling in love
 b) ___ Settling down
 c) ___ Bottoming out
 d) ___ Beginning again

20. Considering that most couples sometimes argue, in an average week, how often would you say that cross words are spoken?
 a) ___ Every day
 b) ___ Three to five times a week
 c) ___ A few times a month
 d) ___ Rarely
 e) ___ Never

21. Do you feel that you and your husband are able to chat with each other as frequently as you would like?

    a) ____ Yes.

    b) ____ No, we need to make more time for conversation.

22. In an average day, how many conversations do you imagine you have with each other?

    a) ____ One or two times

    b) ____ Several times

    c) ____ A lot

23. What would be a rough estimate of the total minutes you converse with your husband during an average day?

    a) ____ 5–10 minutes

    b) ____ 15–30 minutes

    c) ____ 60 minutes or more

24. How many times *a month* do you and your husband make love?

    a) ____ Rarely, if ever

    b) ____ One time or less

    c) ____ Generally less than four times

    d) ____ Probably an average of five to ten times

    e) ____ More

25. Which of the following best describes your feelings about the frequency of your lovemaking?

    a) ____ I would like lovemaking to be more frequent.

    b) ____ It's fine now.

    c) ____ Just not interested.

26. Which describes the level of satisfaction you feel with love-making?

    a) ___ Would like it to be more satisfying.

    b) ___ It is just fine now.

27. Do you agree that there's a correlation between lovemaking and prayer?

    a) ___ I doubt it.

    b) ___ Possibly, but I'm not certain.

    c) ___ I agree, mildly.

    d) ___ I agree, strongly.

28. On a scale of 1 to 10, where would you currently rank your *marital happiness*?

    (1 = very unhappy; 10 = very happy)

_____

29. How often do you and your spouse do the following?

A lot	Sometimes	Rarely	Never	No answer
1	2	3	4	5

a) Hold hands

1	2	3	4	5

b) Laugh together

1	2	3	4	5

c) Go for walks, biking, golf, or other activities

1	2	3	4	5

d) Touch each other fondly

1	2	3	4	5

e) Rub each other's back or feet

1	2	3	4	5

f) Enjoy romantic dates together

1	2	3	4	5

g) Leave love notes to each other

1	2	3	4	5

h) Go to parties together

1	2	3	4	5

i) Enjoy the same music and movies together

1	2	3	4	5

j) Talk privately and lovingly to one another

1	2	3	4	5

k) Ask about each other's work and activities

1	2	3	4	5

l) Go to religious services together

1	2	3	4	5

m) Honor each other respectfully

1	2	3	4	5

n) Really try to understand each other's feelings

| 1 | 2 | 3 | 4 | 5 |

o) Protect your marriage by watching each other's back

| 1 | 2 | 3 | 4 | 5 |

30. Considering where your marriage is right now, where would you rank your fear of divorce?

a) ____ 50/50

b) ____ 25 percent or so

c) ____ 10 percent or so

d) ____ 1 percent or less

31. Some wives like to have girls' night out. Is that something that appeals to you?

a) ____ Appeals to me a lot.

b) ____ Occasionally, it's fun.

c) ____ Rarely, I'd rather be with my spouse.

32. Which answer best describes how you consider your marriage?

a) ____ A married couple doing our best to keep it together

b) ____ Pretty good companions most of the time

c) ____ Best friends with a strong foundation

33. Which best describes your experience with your church or religious organization?

    a) ___ We have received little or no encouragement to pray with each other.

    b) ___ We have heard just a little about praying together.

    c) ___ We have heard some encouragement about this topic.

    d) ___ There has been strong emphasis and encouragement for couples to pray together.

APPENDIX 2

LIFE-CHANGING WISDOM
FROM THE BIBLE

Following are forty passages from the Bible that can be incorporated into your daily prayer. By selecting one of these verses, reading it aloud, then discussing its wisdom and significance to your
contemporary life, you'll enrich your prayer experience.

1. Arguments: Unwholesome Talk
Do not let any unwholesome talk come out of your mouths, but
only what is helpful for building others up . . . Get rid of all bit-
terness, rage and anger . . . along with every form of malice. Be
kind and compassionate to one another.
—Ephesians 4:29, 31–32

2. Argument Avoidance Is Honorable
Keeping away from strife is an honor for a man,
   but any fool will quarrel.
—Proverbs 20:3 NASB

3. Arguments: Avoiding Them Early

Starting a quarrel is like breaching a dam;

so drop the matter before a dispute breaks out.

—Proverbs 17:14

4. Arguments: Patience Is the Antidote

A man's wisdom gives him patience;

it is to his glory to overlook an offense.

—Proverbs 19:11

5. Arguments: Never Go to Bed Angry

We are part of the same body . . . start telling each other the truth . . . Don't go to bed angry and don't give the devil a chance.

—Ephesians 4:25–27 CEV

6. Ask and Imagine

All beings in heaven and on earth receive their life from him. God is wonderful and glorious . . . Stand firm and be deeply rooted in his love . . . His power at work in us can do far more than we dare ask or imagine.

—Ephesians 3:15–17, 21 CEV

7. Ask, Believe, and Receive

If you have faith and do not doubt . . . you can say to this mountain, "Go, throw yourself into the sea," and it will be done. If you believe, you will receive whatever you ask for in prayer.

—Matthew 21:21–22

8. Depending on God

You are a fortress in times of trouble.

Everyone who honors your name can trust you,

    because you are faithful to all who depend on you.

—Psalm 9:9–10 CEV

9. Difficulties

When you go through deep waters and great trouble, I will be with you. When you go through rivers of difficulty, you will not drown! When you walk through the fire of oppression, you will not be burned up; the flames will not consume you.

—Isaiah 43:2 NLT

10. Direction in Your Marriage

Always let him lead you,

    and he will clear the road for you to follow.

—Proverbs 3:6 CEV

11. Discouragement That Prayers Aren't Being Answered

For the revelation awaits an appointed time;

    it speaks of the end and will not prove false.

    Though it linger, wait for it;

    it will certainly come and will not delay.

—Habakkuk 2:3

12. Forgiveness

You must make allowance for each other's faults and forgive the person who offends you. Remember, the Lord forgave you, so you must forgive others. And the most important piece of clothing you must wear is love. Love is what binds us all together in perfect harmony.

—Colossians 3:13–14 NLT

13. Help

I asked the LORD for help,
    and he saved me from all my fears.
Keep your eyes on the LORD! You will shine like the sun
    and never blush with shame.
I was a nobody, but I prayed,
    and the LORD saved me from all my troubles.
If you honor the LORD, his angel will protect you.
Discover for yourself that the LORD is kind.
    Come to him for protection, and you will be glad.
Honor the LORD! You are his special people.
    No one who honors the LORD will ever be in need.
—Psalm 34:4–9 CEV

14. Love: How to Love Each Other

Love is patient, love is kind. It does not envy, it does not boast, it is not proud. It is not rude, it is not self-seeking, it is not easily angered, it keeps no record of wrongs. Love does not delight in evil but rejoices with the truth. It always protects . . . always hopes, always perseveres. Love never fails.

—1 Corinthians 13:4–8

15. Love Your Spouse as You Love Yourself

Husbands ought to love their wives as their own bodies. He who loves his wife loves himself. After all, no one ever hated his own body, but he feeds and cares for it.
—Ephesians 5:28–29

16. Money Issues

No one can serve two masters . . . he will be devoted to the one and despise the other. You cannot serve both God and Money.
—Matthew 6:24

17. Money: Tithing Allows Abundance

Honor the LORD by giving him . . .
    the first part of all your crops.
Then you will have more grain and grapes
    than you will ever need.
—Proverbs 3:9–10 CEV

18. Overcoming

All things work together for good to those who love God.
—Romans 8:28 NKJV

19. Overwhelmed by Uncertainty

Whatever is true, whatever is noble, whatever is right, whatever is pure, whatever is lovely, whatever is admirable . . . think about such things.
—Philippians 4:8

20. Past: Forget Prior History

Forget what happened long ago! Don't think about the past.

I am creating something new.

—Isaiah 43:18–19 CEV

21. Past Indiscretions

Forget the former things;

do not dwell on the past.

—Isaiah 43:18

22. Patience with Each Other

Patience and encouragement . . . come from God [and will] allow you to live in harmony with each other . . . Then you will all be joined together, and you will give glory to God . . . Christ accepted you, so you should accept each other, which will bring glory to God.

—Romans 15:5–7 NCV

23. Plans for Your Life

Many are the plans in a man's heart,

but it is the LORD's purpose that prevails.

—Proverbs 19:21

24. Plans with Hope

For I know the plans I have for you . . . plans to prosper you and not to harm you, plans to give you hope and a future.

—Jeremiah 29:11

25. Power of God

Look at the evening sky! Who created the stars?
  Who gave them each a name? . . .
The LORD is so powerful that none of the stars
  are ever missing.
—Isaiah 40:26 CEV

26. Prayer for Every Need (Lord's Prayer)

Our Father in heaven,
hallowed be your name,
your kingdom come,
your will be done
  on earth as it is in heaven.
Give us today our daily bread.
Forgive us our debts,
  as we also have forgiven our debtors.
And lead us not into temptation,
but deliver us from the evil one.
—Matthew 6:9–13

27. Praying Together

If two of you agree . . . concerning anything you ask, my Father in
heaven will do it for you. For where two or three gather together
because they are mine, I am there among them.
—Matthew 18:19–20 NLT

28. Protection: The Enemy Is Out to Destroy Your Marriage

Put on the full armor of God so that you can take your stand
against the devil's schemes. For our struggle is not against flesh

and blood, but . . . against the spiritual forces of evil in the heavenly realms. Therefore put on the full armor of God, so that when the day of evil comes, you may be able to stand your ground, and after you have done everything, to stand. Stand firm . . . take up the shield of faith, with which you can extinguish all the flaming arrows of the evil one.
—Ephesians 6:11–14, 16

29. Strength

I will keep you safe
    if you turn back to me and calm down.
I will make you strong if you quietly trust me.
—Isaiah 30:15 CEV

30. Succeeding

We humans make plans, but the LORD has the final word.
We may think we know what is right,
    but the LORD is the judge of our motives
Share your plans with the LORD, and you will succeed.
—Proverbs 16:1–3 CEV

31. Support: Holding Your Partner Above Yourself

Are your hearts tender and sympathetic? Then make me truly happy by agreeing wholeheartedly with each other, loving one another, and working together with one heart and purpose.

Don't be selfish; don't live to make a good impression on others. Be humble . . . Don't think only about your own affairs, but be interested in others, too.
—Philippians 2:1–4 NLT

32. Trust: When You Don't Understand What's Happening

With all your heart you must trust the LORD
    and not your own judgment.
Always let him lead you,
    and he will clear the road for you to follow.
—Proverbs 3:5–6 CEV

33. Weakness: Are You Getting Weary?

The LORD is the eternal God, Creator of the earth.
He never gets weary or tired;
    his wisdom cannot be measured.
The LORD gives strength to those who are weary . . .
But those who trust the LORD will find new strength.
They will be strong like eagles soaring upward on wings;
    they will walk and run without getting tired.
—Isaiah 40:28–31 CEV

34. Weak Feelings

My grace is sufficient for you, for my power is made perfect in weakness.
—2 Corinthians 12:9

35. Wisdom

By his wisdom and knowledge
    the LORD created heaven and earth.
By his understanding he let the ocean break loose
    and clouds release the rain.
My child, use common sense and sound judgment!
—Proverbs 3:19–21 CEV

36. Words to Encourage, Not Tear Down
Good people enjoy the positive results of their words.

Those who control their tongue will have a long life; a quick retort can ruin everything.
—Proverbs 13:2–3 NLT

37. Worry Not
Let the peace of Christ rule in your hearts, since as members of one body you were called to peace. And be thankful.
—Colossians 3:15

38. Worry Not About Circumstances in Your Life
Do not worry about anything, but pray and ask God for everything you need, always giving thanks. And God's peace, which is so great we cannot understand it, will keep your hearts and minds in Christ Jesus.
—Philippians 4:6–7 NCV

39. Worry: Looking Past Your Circumstances
So we fix our eyes not on what is seen, but on what is unseen. For what is seen is temporary, but what is unseen is eternal.
—2 Corinthians 4:18

40. Worry and Sleeplessness
You will rest without a worry and sleep soundly.
You can be sure
that the LORD will protect you from harm.
—Proverbs 3:24, 26 CEV

NOTES

Chapter 1: Naked Truth: Marriage's Most Intimate Act

1. Penny Banuchi is cofounder of Marriage and Family Savers Ministries, Newburgh, New York.

2. Andrew Greeley, *Faithful Attraction* (New York: TOR, 1991), 292.

3. Ibid., 229.

4. "Summary of Faithful Attraction Data," October 9, 2007, Byron Johnson and Jerry Park, Baylor University Institute for Studies of Religion.

5. Steve Carr, "How Prayer Builds Your Marriage," Covenant Keepers, www.covenantkeepers.org/articles/prayer.htm, accessed 14 Jan 2007.

6. Greeley, *Faithful Attraction*, 230.

7. Robert Schuller, "Ten Tips for Making Marriage Fun," New Hope, www.newhopenow.com/schuller/marriage/sermon_31.html, accessed 14 Sept 2007.

8. Jack W. Hayford, *Living the Spirit-Filled Life* (Nashville: Thomas Nelson, 1994).

Chapter 2: Prayer and Communication

1. Deborah Tannen, *You Just Don't Understand: Women and Men in Conversation* (New York: William Morrow, 1990), 24.

2. Adrienne Broaddus, "Broadway play helps sexes understand each other," *The State News*, www.defendingthecaveman.com/04-reviews.html, accessed 8 Sept 2007.

3. Warren Gerds, "*Caveman* delivers laugh after laugh," posted 17 Sept 2003, www.defendingthecaveman.com/04-reviews.html, accessed 8 Sept 2007.

4. Elizabeth Clark, "*Defending the Caveman* takes us back to the basics," Special to the *Gazette*, 22 Oct 2003. Review 2003 Kalamazoo. Used with permission. www.defendingthecaveman.com/04-reviews.html, accessed 8 Sept 2007.

5. Michael McManus, "His Needs, Her Needs," Ethics & Religion, 3 July 2007, www.ethicsandreligion.com/redesignedcolumns/C1349.htm.

6. Tannen, *You Just Don't Understand*, 288.

7. Ibid.

8. Matthew 18:20.

9. Andrew Greeley, *Faithful Attraction* (New York: TOR, 1991), 67.

Chapter 3: The 40 Day Prayer Challenge™

1. Rick Warren, *The Purpose Driven Life* (Grand Rapids: Zondervan Publishing Company, 2007), 7.

Chapter 4: How Do You Do It?

1. Based on a true story; names have been changed.

2. Elisabeth Sifton, *The Serenity Prayer* (New York: W. W. Norton & Company, 2003).

Chapter 5: The Remarkable Power of Prayer

1. Lee Strobel, *The Case for a Creator* (Grand Rapids: Zondervan Publishing Company, 2004).

2. Ibid.

3. "Profile: Dr. Francis Collins," *Religion and Ethics Newsweekly* (Public Broadcasting System), 21 July 2006, episode 947, www.pbs.org/wnet/religionandethics/week947/profile.html.

4. Francis Collins, *The Language of God* (New York: Free Press, 2006), 1–2.

5. Ibid., 20.

6. Ibid., 23.

7. Ibid., 25.

8. Ibid., 30.

9. Ibid., 66–67.

10. Harold G. Koenig, David B. Larson, Michael E. McCullough, *Handbook of Religion and Health* (New York: Oxford University Press, 2001).

11. Kathleen Fackelmann, "The Power of Prayer Six-Year Study Suggests People Can Be Blessed with Longer Lives," *USA Today*, July 18, 2000.

12. "Prayer and Healing," DukeMedNews, 30 Nov 2001, www.dukemednews.org/av/medminute.php?id=5136.

13. Randolph C. Byrd, MD, "Positive Therapeutic Effects of

Intercessory Prayer in a Coronary Care Unit Population," *Southern Medical Journal,* vol. 81, no. 7, 826–29.

14. Based on a true story; names have been changed.

15. Scott Hamilton, *Landing It* (New York: Kesington Publishing Corp., 1999), 38.

16. Scott Hamilton interview with SQuire Rushnell, 21 February 2007.

17. Academy of Achievement, Achiever Gallery, Scott Hamilton, Profile, www.achievement.org/autodoc/page/ham0pro-1.

18. Scott Hamilton interview with SQuire Rushnell, 21 February 2007.

19. Hamilton, *Landing It,* 454.

20. F. F. Bruce, *The Books and the Parchments* (Old Tappan, NJ: Revell, 1963), 78.

21. F. F. Bruce, *The New Testament Documents: Are They Reliable?* (Downers Grove, IL: InterVarsity Press, 1971), 15.

22. Robert C. Newman, "Miracles and the Historicity of the Easter Week Narratives," in John Warwick Montgomery (ed.) , *Evidence for Faith: Deciding the God Question* (Dallas: Probe, 1991), 284.

23. Paul Little, *Certainty: Know Why You Believe* (Downers Grove, IL: InterVarsity Press, 1996).

Chapter 6: The Devil Is a Real Enemy of Your Marriage

1. Ryan Singel, "Internet Porn: Worse than Crack?," *Wired* magazine, www.wired.com/science/discoveries/news/2004/11/65772, 19 November 2004.

2. Dr. Mary Anne Layden, "Testimony for US Senate Committee on Commerce, Science and Transportation," 18 Nov

2004, www.obscenitycrimes.org/Senate-Reisman-Layden-Etc.pdf, accessed 21 Sept 2007.

Chapter 7: Forgiveness Power

1. Mark 11:25 NLT.

2. Matthew 6:11–12 NKJV.

3. See Matthew 18:21–22.

4. Brainyquote.com, s.v. "Carrie Fisher," accessed 25 May 2007.

5. Paula Friedrichsen, *The Man You Always Wanted Is the One You Already Have* (Colorado Springs: Multnomah Publishers, 2006), 19.

6. Brainy Quote, Henry Ward Beecher Quotes, www.brainyquote.com/quotes/authors/h/henry_ward_beecher.html.

Chapter 8: Prayer and Money

1. *American Heritage Dictionary of the English Language, Third Edition* (Boston: Houghton Mifflin Company, 1992).

2. David Kuo, "Rick Warren's Second Reformation," Beliefnet.com, www.beliefnet.com/story/177/story_17718_1.html, accessed 23 Aug 2007.

3. Steve Pavlina, "Tithing," StevePavlina.com, 15 Nov 2005, www.stevepavlina.com/blog/2005/11tithing, accessed 15 Oct 2007.

Chapter 9: Six Steps to a Happy Marriage

1. Brainy Quote, Bill Cosby Quotes, www.brainyquote.com/quotes/quotes/b/billcosby131321.html, accessed 9 Oct 2007.

2. "Silly Little Green Froggy" is adapted with permission

from the original *Guideposts* magazine story "Surprised by Love" by Linda Gillis, © 2007, Carmel, NY: Guideposts. All rights reserved.

3. Jackie Chew, "A Laugh a Day Keeps the Doctor Away?" Serendip, www.serendip.brynmawr.edu/biology/b103/f01/web2/ chew.html, accessed 10 Oct 2007.

4. www.longevity.about.com/b/a/000107.htm, accessed 14 Oct 2007.

5. Brainyquote.com, s.v. "Alan Cohen," accessed 28 Aug 2007.

6. John Wooden, *Wooden* (New York: McGraw-Hill, 1997), 19.

7. Ibid., 18.

Those extraordinary little events in your life happen for a reason.

A COINCIDENCE—SOMETIMES A SILLY LITTLE THING
—CHANGES THE COURSE OF YOUR DAY . . .
OR EVEN YOUR LIFE. IS IT CHANCE, IS IT LUCK,
OR IS GOD COMMUNICATING WITH YOU?

WHEN GOD WINKS AT YOU
ISBN 978-0-7852-1892-0

When God Winks at You is packed with true stories demonstrating that God *does* communicate with us, making incredible things happen in our lives every single day. As you read the riveting accounts of everyday and famous people—including Tim Conway, Rudolph Giuliani, Billy Graham, and Don Knotts—you will begin to recognize the *godwinks* in your own life, both past and present. Through these tangible signposts from God, we receive personalized messages that reassure us, stop us from worrying, chart our path in life, and help us keep the faith.

When God winks, He is reaffirming that there is absolutely nothing about us that He does not know—our every hurt, our every desire. And that to me is very comforting.
—SQuire Rushnell